P9-CRR-119

BARNES & NOBLE BASICS™

golf

by Blaine Newnham

BARNES & NOBLE
BOOKS
NEW YORK

Copyright © 2003 by Silver Lining Books,
an imprint of Barnes & Noble, Inc.

ISBN 076074128x

All rights reserved. No part of this book may be reproduced or
transmitted in any form or by any electronic or mechanical
means, including information storage and retrieval systems,
without permission in writing, with the exception of brief
passages used in a critical article or review.

First Edition
Printed and bound in the United States of America

While Silver Lining Books and the author have used best efforts in writing this book,
they make no representations or warranties as to its accuracy and completeness.
They also do not make any implied warranties of merchantability or fitness for a particular purpose. Any advice given in this book is not guaranteed or warranted and it
may not be suitable for every factual situation. Neither Silver Lining Books nor the
author shall be liable for any losses suffered by any reader of this book.

This book offers a summary of some of *The Rules of Golf* and the *USGA Handicap System
Manual* as interpreted by the author. It does not carry the official approval of the USGA,
which does not therefore warrant the accuracy of the author's interpretations. Readers
should refer to the full text of the *Rules* and *Handicap Manual* as published in the official
publications, *The Rules of Golf*, published by the USGA/R&A, and *Handicap System
Manual*, published by the USGA.

For information, contact:
Silver Lining Books
122 Fifth Avenue
New York, NY 10011
212-633-4000

Other titles in the **Barnes & Noble Basics**™ series:
Barnes & Noble Basics *Using Your PC*
Barnes & Noble Basics *Wine*
Barnes & Noble Basics *In the Kitchen*
Barnes & Noble Basics *Getting in Shape*
Barnes & Noble Basics *Saving Money*
Barnes & Noble Basics *Getting a Job*
Barnes & Noble Basics *Using the Internet*
Barnes & Noble Basics *Retiring*
Barnes & Noble Basics *Using Your Digital Camera*
Barnes & Noble Basics *Getting Married*
Barnes & Noble Basics *Grilling*
Barnes & Noble Basics *Giving a Presentation*
Barnes & Noble Basics *Buying a House*
Barnes & Noble Basics *Volunteering*
Barnes & Noble Basics *Getting a Grant*
Barnes & Noble Basics *Getting into College*

introduction

"I know you can't just pick up a club and start swinging, but I don't want to take forever to learn to play golf. There has to be a way into this game without too much pain and suffering," exclaimed my good friend Mike C.

There is an easier way. Whether your golf experience has just meant watching Tiger Woods on TV or you've actually hit a few forgettable buckets of balls at the local golf range, you'll find everything here to get you into this well-loved sport. Inside these easy-to-understand, beautifully illustrated pages you'll learn the right way to grip a club, common tee-off errors, course etiquette, the proper stance, ways to improve accuracy, all-important mental tips (most people agree golf is as much a mental game as a physical one), tips to lower your score, and much, much more. Want to know the difference between a birdie and an eagle? Turn to page 41. Want to know how to avoid a slice? See page 108. How to use a sand wedge? Page 132.

Yes, golf is a game unto itself, but you now have the key to unlock its joys and wonders. Just turn these pages and the game is yours. Fore!

Barb Chintz
Editorial Director, the **Barnes & Noble Basics**™ series

table of contents

Chapter 1 Why Golf? 6
The romance of the game 8   How the game works 10
Golf clubs 12   The handicap 14   Golf lessons 16   The pros
on the tour 18   Now what do I do? 20

Chapter 2 Where to Play 22
Driving ranges 24   Public courses 26   "Public" private
courses 28   Country club courses 30   Resort courses 32
Now what do I do? 34

Chapter 3 The Golf Course 36
18-hole courses 38   Par for the course 40   The tee 42
The fairway 44   Hazards 46   The putting green 48   Course
ratings 50   Now what do I do? 52

Chapter 4 On the Course 54
The rule book 56   When problems arise 58   Course etiquette 60
Respecting the course 62   The golf cart 64   Walking the
course 66   Types of local matches 68   Country club tournaments 70   Playing it safe 72   Now what do I do? 74

Chapter 5 Equipment 76
Woods 78   Irons 80   Wedges 82   Putters 84   Golf balls 86
Golf shoes and gloves 88   Golf clothes and accessories 90
Now what do I do? 92

Chapter 6 Teeing Off 94
Using the driver 96   The grip 98   The stance 100   The back-
swing 102   The downswing 104   The follow through 106
Common tee-off errors 108   Now what do I do? 110

Chapter 7 The Fairway Shot 112
Using the irons 114   The short irons 116   The stance 118
The swing 120   Difficult lies 122   Now what do I do? 124

Chapter 8 The Approach Shot 126
The chip shot 128   The pitch shot 130   Using the sand
wedge 132   Now what do I do? 134

Chapter 9 The Putt 136
On the green 138   Lining up the putt 140   The grip and
stance 142   The right stroke 144   Controlling distance 146
Improving accuracy 148   Now what do I do? 150

Chapter 10 Improving Your Game 152
Fixing the slice 154   Fixing the hook 156   Improper backswing 158   Hitting too low and too high 160   Poor putting 162
How to practice 164   Overcoming golf anxiety 166   Mental
tips 168   Tips to lower your score 170   Competition dos and
don'ts 172   Gambling 174   Now what do I do? 176

Chapter 11 Fitting Golf In 178
Golf on the road 180   Business golf 182   Golf vacations 184
Irish and Scottish courses 186   Teaching kids 188   Now what
do I do? 190

Glossary 192

Index 196

Chapter 1

Why Golf?

The romance of the game 8
A grand game with a rich history

How the game works 10
From tee to green

Golf clubs 12
What they do

The handicap 14
Why golf is open to all

Golf lessons 16
Let a teaching pro help you get started

The pros on the tour 18
The hard-won glamour of the game

Now what do I do? 20
Answers to common questions

HOW A PRO WOULD PLAY IT

Difficult par 5
585 yards

"I'd hit my drive as far as I could toward the left side. I'd use a long iron for my second shot and try to bounce the ball onto the green."

the romance of the game

A captivating sport

Can you imagine practicing your golf swing with an imaginary club while you wait at the checkout line at a store? Or sleeping overnight in your car for the chance to play one of the top ten golf courses in the world? Or driving all over creation to get the perfect putter? It happens all the time to a fun but devoted group of sportspeople known as golfers. For them, golf is a mystical sport.

With golf, it doesn't matter how big or strong you are, nor how young or old; the game of golf is beyond the mere physical. It's

about community: Children can play with adults; amateurs can play with professionals. It's about overcoming personal obstacles, whether it's doubt about your ability to play well or trepidation at approaching a really tough hole.

Most who try their hand at golf end up loving it. How does that happen? Your first really good shot on a golf course is what does it. You'll amaze yourself with how high and far the ball goes, often against a backdrop of

tall trees or rustling grasses. What gets you is how effortless it felt. Alas, you may go for weeks or years trying to imitate that shot, that feeling of overarching achievement. The challenge never ends. That's because with golf, unlike other competitive sports, you're always playing against yourself. If you're lucky, golf will turn you into a worthy opponent. One who enjoys the thrill of the game but can also savor the beauty of an early morning when your putt turns heavy dew into a rooster tail on the grass and your ball sinks into the cup and the world stands still, if only for one glorious moment.

The History of a Grand Game

The appeal and addiction of golf has been with us for centuries. Back in 1457, King James II of Scotland issued an act of Parliament banning golf because his subjects were playing too much golf and neglecting their archery practice. But not even a royal decree could stop this game. The first golf club, the Royal and Ancient Golf Club of St. Andrews, was founded in Scotland in 1754. Since then golf has been taken up all over the world, nowhere more so than in the United States.

The first American golf club was founded in 1888 in Yonkers, New York, and the sport was quickly embraced by the Yanks. No one propelled the game of golf more than the American Bobby Jones, who, as an amateur, won all the major championships by age 30 and went on to found Augusta National Golf Course, home of the Masters Championship.

The United States Golf Association (USGA) was established in 1894, and the first official tournament was created, namely the U.S. Open. When the major tournaments of golf were first televised in the 1960s, golf exploded on the scene, and quite a few golfers became household names. There was Arnold Palmer, whose cool confidence during championships and good nature won him millions of fans who refer to him simply as Arnie. Jack Nicklaus, dubbed "the golden bear," is another favorite. The names roll on: Raymond Floyd, Tom Watson, Lee Trevino, Greg Norman, and Nick Price. Nothing, however, prepared the golf world for the impact of Tiger Woods, a young professional who has won all the major tournaments and whose grace and athleticism have inspired awe in rivals and fans alike.

American women have been playing golf since the beginning of the last century. They owe a great debt to the phenomenal athlete Babe Zaharias, who helped found the Ladies Professional Golf Association in the 1940s. Again, thanks to television, women pros have earned a place in the golf hall of fame. Some favorites are Karrie Webb, an exceptionally strong player who has won numerous tournaments. She can drive the ball an average of 250 yards. Such talent has done much to dispel the myth that women golfers are great at the short shots but can't hit the ball very far. Women's golf entered a new phase of competition with the record-breaking scores of Annika Sorenstam, a top-ranked women's pro golfer. She shot a 59 to win one tournament.

how the game works

From tee to green

Golf is a simple game. It's played on a course that typically has 18 holes. The goal is to get the golf ball from each **tee** (where each hole begins) to the little **hole** (the small metal-lined **cup** that's sunk about six inches into the **green**, or putting surface, at the end of each hole) in as few strokes as possible. A **stroke** is counted when the club is moved forward with the intention of making contact with the ball. A stroke is counted even if no contact is made and the ball doesn't move after a swing. It's the intent that counts.

An excellent player averages **par** for each hole. What's par? It's the number of strokes a top player should take to get the ball from the tee into the hole. On long holes, the par is 5; on short holes it's 3; and on average-length holes it's 4. How many strokes does an excellent golfer need to complete a standard 18-hole golf course? The average is about 72 strokes. This is known as **par for the course**. Achieving par for the course—the ideal golf round—is so difficult that only excellent golfers manage to do it consistently.

Most golfers need far more than 72 strokes. They're happy with "bogey" golf—which means they take on average one more shot than par on each hole—a five instead of a four on a par-4 hole. Instead of scoring a 72, their score is in the 90s or higher.

ASK THE EXPERTS

How long does a round last?

On a typical course with 18 holes, the average round takes four to four and a half hours. If there are a lot of players on the course, a round may take longer. For that reason, some people opt to play only nine holes or half the course at a time. Nine holes will usually take you two hours or so.

How is the score kept?

Before you go out to play a round of golf, you'll need a scorecard (which gives you information about the course and lets you record your score) and a pencil. Both normally sit on the counter in the **golf shop**, where the golf pro usually resides and where you can purchase golf equipment and pay your **greens fee** (the cost of play-ing a round of golf). The scorecard will have a space for scores of up to four players, as golf is normally played in groups of four, or a **foursome**. Before you start to play, usually one person is elected to keep tally of the scores. At the end of each hole, you report your score on the hole to the scorekeeper, who will trust what you say because you're expected to count all the strokes. At the end of the game, the scorekeeper adds up each player's score for the 18 holes.

How do the great golfers manage to make par on a hole?

Ideally, their first stroke hits the ball from the tee (the starting position of each hole) out onto the **fairway**, the landing area between the tee and the putting green. The next shot is called the **approach**. With great golfers, their approach shots nearly always land on the green. That leaves them one or two strokes to putt. Count it all up and you have four shots from tee to cup.

golf clubs

Start with a starter set

Your golf club is basically a long shaft with a clubhead at one end and a grip at the other. You hold the club at the grip and hit the ball with the face of that clubhead. Sounds pretty simple. If only it were! Hitting that little ball with precision and power is very tricky indeed. Moreover, because the goal is to make as few strokes as possible, you'll need different clubs as you get closer to the hole. And you'll need special clubs to deal with all the fun things you're sure to encounter on a golf course, such as ponds, sand, and tall grass. That's why a regulation set of clubs most often consists of 14 different clubs—three woods, eight irons, two wedges, and one putter. (More on all these clubs on pages 78–85.)

If you're just starting, don't just borrow or rent any old set of clubs. Look for clubs that fit you. They should be the right length, their shafts should have flexibility to match your strength, and the grips should be the right size for your hands. Who can give you advice on what is the right fit for you? Ideally, those selling or renting the clubs. Check with the pro (see page 16) at the golf course you're playing or the person running the driving range (see page 24) for golf club advice.

A standard starter set includes five to six irons (one of which can be a pitching wedge), two woods, and a putter (not shown here).

To ensure a proper swing, make sure your starter clubs fit you. You want clubs that allow for the proper stance (middle). Clubs that are too short (left) will cause you to bend too far over; clubs that are too long (right) will force you to choke down on the club; both will make it more difficult to make a good swing.

Buying Your First Set

What do you really need when you're first starting out in golf? Start smart with a **starter set**. You can purchase a starter set for $300 or less. These sets include two woods (which are now made out of metal), four to five irons, a wedge, and a putter. You want the clubs to fit your hand as well as your body. Pros in the shops at every golf course can help ensure that your clubs are the proper length and have the right flexibility in the shafts and the right-size grips. Sometimes they'll charge a small fee for the service and then waive the fee if you buy your clubs from them. Once you know what you need, your options become endless. You can get the clubs at pro shops, sporting goods stores, from catalogues, or on the Internet. For more information on clubs, see pages 78–85.

the handicap

Golf's great equalizer

Unlike most major competitive sports, golf has a formal **handicap** system that allows players to compete with one another no matter what their skill level might be. What handicapping does is to equalize the abilities of each player. How is this done? Through a little bit of math wizardry. In golf, the handicap is a number that technically allows a player to reach par, if only mathematically.

How do you get a handicap? First you need to join some kind of golf group—most golf courses have men's and women's groups. These groups take care of submitting your scores, usually via a handicap computation service. The computer factors in the difficulty of the courses you've played, compiles your scores, and then tabulates your handicap. Your club will then issue you a handicap index. Here's a very simplistic example: If you consistently shot 100 for 18 holes and the par for the course you play is 72, then your handicap would be 28 (100-72=28).

With this handicap you can even compete against a pro and stand a chance of winning. How so? If you play against a pro with a 0, or **scratch**, handicap, you would get the benefit of a 28-stroke advantage before you ever hit the ball off the first tee. If you shoot a 98 and your opponent shoots 72, you would win by two strokes. Thanks to the handicapping system, golf lets you compete against others, no matter whether you've been playing for years or have just begun.

ASK THE EXPERTS

Why can't I calculate my own handicap and save the bother of applying for an official handicap?

While it might seem as if an official handicap is a bit overzealous, it keeps the game honest. Your buddies may trust your homegrown estimates, but new opponents may not. With a handicap index, you'll never have to guess. And if you faithfully and accurately report your scores, you will be able to tee up in a fair competition with anyone who does the same. You'll also be able to keep track of your own progress.

What keeps people from putting in wrong scores to raise their handicap?

The integrity that goes with the spirit of the game, along with the club's handicap committee, which monitors score posting and maintains the integrity of the USGA Handicap System. There is no referee on the golf course. Unlike other sports, where athletes sometimes try to take advantage of the rules until caught, the golfer is expected to police himself. A few misguided people want handicaps that are higher than they should be so that they have an unfair advantage. Those culprits are called **sandbaggers**. They want to win so badly that they will fail to report their best scores, or waste easy shots just so their scores will be worse than they should be. You don't want to be one of them.

What is the highest and lowest handicap index?

For men, the highest handicap for which the USGA will officially issue a certificate is 36.4; for women the highest handicap is 40.4. While it would make sense that the lowest handicap would be par or 0 (also known as **scratch**), some players are so good that they shoot better than par. For a really fine player, his handicap then goes into the plus numbers, as in +3 handicap. This means the player gives strokes back to the course. A player with a +3 handicap who shot a 69 would then have to add three strokes for a 72 as his official score.

golf lessons

Turning your game around

Okay, you've hit some balls on the driving range and put some time into practicing on a putting green. You're pretty sure this game is for you. Now what? Before you go out on a course, try some golf lessons. Golf lessons from a teaching pro can make all the difference in your game. Most teaching pros are affiliated with a private or public golf course or a driving range. You don't necessarily need to be a member of the pro's club to have lessons.

Most teaching pros belong to the Professional Golfers Association (PGA). Look for the PGA certification in the office. This pro's certificate means they have successfully met a playing test by shooting a certain score. They've also passed a written test that rates their knowledge of the game and have worked at a golf club under a PGA member for at least three years. They know their stuff.

The question is whether they can pass their knowledge on to you. That's why you'll need references from friends, preferably ones who are good golfers. Ask them specifically how the pro improved their game. Once you've narrowed down the field of choices, interview several pros. One question to ask is whether they ever give lessons on the course, helping to explain rules and etiquette along the way.

Like many teaching pros, Carl Alexander (of the GlenArbor Golf Club in Bedford, New York) can videotape your swing to pinpoint the errors of your ways and help you correct your form.

You want to make sure the pro has the equipment to diagnose the problems in your swing. Some pros use videocameras to tape your swing and show you your errors. Next consider the pro's facilities. Is there access to a range, a practice sand trap, a practice putting green? Ideally, a pro has access to all three. Another option—try a golf vacation and load up on lessons while enjoying a new course complete with all the amenities. (See page 184 for more.) Or consider signing up for golf camp. These are available for adult as well as junior golfers. (See page 189 for more.)

ASK THE EXPERTS

What happens in group lessons?

Turning your golf swing over to someone, even a teaching professional, can leave you feeling vulnerable. There's safety in numbers. Think about signing up for a group lesson, preferably with those of similar needs. A group lesson is usually less expensive than an individual lesson. For one thing, it can give you a chance to watch your pro at work in a less intense and expensive setting. The problems experienced by others trying to execute their swing should help keep you from being embarrassed by what you do. The struggle is all around you. Try to get in a group lesson that both matches your ability and meets your needs. There might be one just on chipping, for example, and others on putting, or hitting out of the sand, or using a wedge. The group lesson also gives you a little more time to adjust and practice what is being taught before the instructor singles you out for help—and maybe even praise.

I want my children to learn the game. How old should they be to start?

That's a tricky one. Tiger Woods started when he was two years old. His father cut adult clubs down to fit him and then taught him how to swing them. The rest is history. Many children come into contact with golf through miniature golf. This is a fun introduction to putting. Young children, say, seven years old and up, can start to learn how to swing the other clubs. Most driving ranges have clubs for children; quite a few have after-school programs for kids. Let them try out the sport there. If they like it, try a pitch and putt course or a par 3-course. Once they really show an interest, sign them up for lessons. Since children often prefer activities with their peers, group golf lessons for children are a great way to start learning about the game.

the pros on the tour

Not just putting around

Chances are your first introduction to golf came while watching a golf tournament on television. There are many professional golf tournaments. The pros who play on the tournament circuit, or tour, usually are not teaching pros. The competition between the pros on the tour for these tournaments is fierce. They make their living by winning the prize money or endorsing golf products for the corporate sponsors who help defray their cost of competing.

Avid golf spectators on the roof of the restrooms at Bethpage State Park Golf Course on Long Island, New York, during the 2002 U.S. Open.

Like any other major sport, golf has a number of competitions that are televised worldwide. There are four major tournaments in golf each year: the U.S. Open, the Masters, the PGA Championship, and the British Open. Each tournament comes with a large **purse**, or prize money. Very few pros have managed to win all of them in their career. Once a pro on the circuit turns 50, he or she has the option to join the Senior PGA or Senior LPGA and compete in their tournaments as well as the PGA tournaments.

ASK THE EXPERTS

Do women pros have their own tournaments?

Yes, they do. For women pros, the majors are the Kraft Nabisco Championship, the LPGA Championship, the U.S. Women's Open, and the Women's British Open. These tournaments are usually televised, and the purse (prize money) is steadily growing, as is women's golf.

Why do women pros play separate tournaments from the men?

Tradition. But that's changing. Technology has helped women hit the ball far enough to play the toughest courses. Just as women are assuming bigger roles in business, so they are on the country's golf courses and in professional golf associations. In 2003 a woman is going to play in a PGA tour event for the first time. The growth in women's golf has prompted changes in golf courses—such as adding more appropriate tees—brought about golf-for-women magazines, and increased interest in women's professional golf.

Why do pros always use caddies during tournaments?

It's a tradition of the sport as well as a requirement on all major tours. In professional golf, caddies do more than just carry the clubs. They walk the course before the tournament and mark off the distances. Often caddies offer advice about the hole and selection of club. Some pros have the same caddie for their entire careers.

FIRST PERSON DISASTER STORY

Eyes open, mouth shut

It was the first time I ever saw a pro tournament in person. I got right up in the front of the gallery, as the fans are called, and got to see these pros as they teed off on the first hole. Wow, what action. They could really belt that ball. I was so impressed by one shot that I yelled out, "Nice one." I guess I was a little too loud, and some official came over and told me there was no talking during shots. The members of the gallery could talk only after all the players had teed off, and not before.

—Sam T., Wayne, New Jersey

now what do I do?

Just how important are lessons?

Nothing is more important to a beginner than lessons. A golfer who has been taught how to swing correctly with the right grip can hit shots with even the worst clubs. The reverse is not true. Expensive clubs won't help a bad swing. A bad grip never gets better. Get started the right way and take lessons.

Who can I play golf with when I don't know any golfers?

If you're just starting out, go to a golf range and practice hitting first. (See page 24.) Once you can hit all the various types of golf shots that are required on a course (the tee shot, the long iron, the short iron, and the putt), you can consider playing on a golf course. Chances are you won't be able to play by yourself. Instead, the **starter**—the course official who controls who gets on the course— will team you up with other individuals or groups of three or less. You'll be put in a group of up to four people.

I've never played on a course before. What should I do?

Your golfing partners will expect that you have a basic understanding of the rules and can keep up with them. So will all of the groups that follow you. That's why you might want your first trip around a course to be with a friend who knows the game. Go in the late afternoon when the serious players are finished playing. Have your friend walk you through each hole and point out the type of shots you should take and what rules and etiquette to observe. (For more on rules and etiquette see pages 56–61.) You can also hire a golf pro to walk you around the course (though that can be a bit pricey). You'll get to learn tips and rules while you play, which will make you more comfortable when placed with strangers.

What about golf shoes and a golf glove?

The golf shoes most people wear these days no longer have metal spikes. They have rubber spikes, called soft spikes. Many courses demand them because they do less damage to the course. Some of the new shoes look like sneakers. You can actually wear sneakers, and except under the wettest conditions they'll be fine. A golf glove can improve your grip and keep you from getting blisters, but the truth is you shouldn't grip the club so tightly that you get blisters.

How can I feel comfortable around experienced golfers when there are so many rules to learn?

While golf has strict rules and a long history, the game is more about respect than it is about rules. Experienced golfers love the game. They want you to share in that passion by showing respect for the course and for other golfers. If you are uncertain about what to do, simply ask your fellow players. They'll be glad to share their knowledge.

Why are some people so crazy about golf?

Perhaps because it's such a multifaceted game. It's social—since it takes four-plus hours to play, you get a chance to really talk to your fellow players, be they friends or family. But you can also play alone (try that with tennis). Golf is challenging but forgiving; it's a hard game to master, but the beauty is that you get a fresh start with each new shot. So even if you have a bad couple of holes, there's always hope for improvement. Golf is played in a beautiful setting—usually 18 holes of rolling countryside. Playing a game is often the only time some people spend outside in the fresh air. Finally, it is a game that anyone can play—young, old, big, small, strong, or weak.

Helpful Resources

WEB SITES

www.USGA.org
The United States Golf Association

golf.about.com/library/weekly/aa110202a.htm
Helpful hints for the beginning golfer

PUBLICATIONS

The PGA Manual of Golf
by Rick Martino

The Golf Fitness Handbook
by Gary Wiren

The Women's Guide to Golf
by Kellie Stenzel Garvin

Golf for Dummies
by Gary McCord

The Majors: In Pursuit of Golf's Holy Grail
by John Feinstein

Chapter 2

Where to Play

Driving ranges 24
The best places to begin

Public courses 26
Municipal courses are easier and cheaper

"Public" private courses 28
Almost a country club

Country club courses 30
Membership has its privileges

Resort courses 32
Spectacular courses to test your skills

Now what do I do? 34
Answers to common questions

HOW A PRO
WOULD PLAY IT

Easy par 4
400 yards

"This is definitely a birdie opportunity. I'd hit my tee shot straight down the middle."

driving ranges

Home on the range

Welcome to the perfect place to practice golf: the **driving range**. It's typically a rectangular-shaped practice area that's either indoors or out in the open, usually 300 yards long. On one side of the range there are usually 10 to 20 little practice hitting areas, each 10 feet in diameter or more, so there is room to swing a club without gettting in the way of the person on either side of you. Think of these hitting areas as your personal batting cage.

Okay, you are ready to try your hand at practicing on a range. How does it work? You pay the range operator for practice balls, often getting a bucket of 50 for $5 and 100 for $7.50. (You just hit them onto the range; the range owner picks them up later and rents them again.) Usually you'll find golf clubs to use for free or for rent. With golf clubs and a bucket of balls in hand, simply find a free spot and start. You can take as long or as short a time as you want to hit all your balls.

The good news is that on a range you're free from intimidation. No one really watches what you do. It's just you and a bucket of balls. You can practice any type of shot you want (except for putting). You can work on your drive as well as your long and short iron swing. And you can track your distance—most ranges have distance markers or flags so you can tell how far you're hitting the ball.

Public driving ranges come in all shapes and sizes and levels of sophistication, from outdoor open ranges set in cow pastures to city ranges on piers with river views (as above). There are also multitiered indoor facilities, some of which have computers to track your shots. TIP: Be sure to practice all the different types of shots you need on the course, from the drive to the pitch shot.

ASK THE EXPERTS

Can I go to a driving range and just start without any lessons?

Sure! You can borrow one of the range's golf clubs, offered for free or for rent, and try hitting the ball. If you swing and miss the ball, don't worry. Try again. You could also bring a golfer friend to show you some basics, or ask the range staff to give you pointers about how to pick the right-size club and how to hold it. That said, a number of golf ranges offer lessons. (More on golf lessons on page 16.)

Do I need to bring golf shoes or anything else?

Golf shoes, no; a golf glove, maybe. Bring a golf glove (see page 88) to the range because it will help your grip (how you hold the golf club) and prevent you from getting blisters. (See more about grip on page 98.) It's perfectly fine to wear sneakers.

How often should I practice at a range?

That depends entirely on you. Beginning golfers should try to hit the range every weekend for a good half hour or more. That said, some golf enthusiasts go every few nights after work. It's a great way to get rid of stress. Since most 18-hole golf courses have their own driving ranges, it's also a good idea to warm up with a bucket of balls before you play a round of golf.

FIRST PERSON DISASTER STORY

Home on the Range

My big brother had always wanted me to try my hand at golf. One afternoon, I thought I'd surprise him and try hitting some balls at a driving range. I borrowed a couple of clubs at the range and bought a bucket of balls, and off I went. There was something wonderful about whacking that little ball to the far wall of the range. I had a blast until I realized that my right shoulder was aching and I was getting a blister on my hand. I sheepishly mentioned this to my brother, who said that you should do warm-up swings to get your back loosened up and switch clubs so you don't stress your back and shoulders with the same shot over and over again. And that you should always use a golf glove when you hit at a range. Big brothers still know best.

—Ted M., Sioux City, Iowa

public courses

Getting the most for your tax dollars

Contrary to popular opinion, golf is not an elite sport. In fact, 80 percent of golf in the United States is played on courses open to the public. Some of these are owned by local or state governments, hence their name, **municipal courses**, or munis. Some good news: Most older munis were built without a lot of hazards and sand traps, making them a natural starting course for beginners. Even better news: A number of municipal courses are amazing. The U.S. Open in 2002 was played on Bethpage Black, a municipal course on Long Island, New York.

Some towns don't have room for a full-blown 18-hole course, so they opt for the 9-hole muni. These courses are ideal for a beginner because they cost less in greens fees and take less time to play.

One way to keep the cost down for a round of golf is to walk and avoid the charge for a golf cart.

Since munis are municipally owned, they often give preference to local taxpayers. By proving your residence, you get a card from the parks and recreation department or the municipal course itself that entitles you to a form of membership. You can play a round of golf for a vastly reduced **greens fee**, or price—say $15 to $30 for 18 holes. (Nonresidents will be charged at a different rate.) Just as important, you can call and reserve a time to play (known as a **tee time**).

ASK THE EXPERTS

What's an executive course?

This is a short 9- or 18-hole course. The majority of holes are short par 3s. These usually range in distance from 75 yards to 175 yards. These executive courses take less time to play and are more forgiving of missed shots. Still, they let you practice plenty of important shots. You'll get a lot of chances to **chip** (a shot of relatively short distance meant to get the ball as close to the hole as possible) and **pitch** (hit the ball that's on the fringe of the green toward the hole).

How do I prove I'm a resident in my town so I can play on its municipal golf course?

Simple. Call the golf course or your town's recreation office and ask what form of identification is required. Usually, a tax bill or electrical bill will suffice, plus a picture ID. Bring those to the golf course office and fill out the required forms. You typically have to pay a yearly fee, anywhere from $20 to $200. Once that's paid, you pay a nominal greens fee when you play. (Nonresidents have to pay a much higher greens fee.)

How do I go about playing on a municipal golf course?

You need to call the municipal golf course (they usually have an office at the course) and ask for an available tee time. The times are available on a first-come, first-served basis and open to the public—residents and nonresidents alike. The difference is that residents will pay lower greens fees than out-of-towners, and they usually get first crack at tee times. It's best to call a few weeks in advance if you want to play on the weekends. You may also find that some munis do not reserve tee times and people play on a first-come basis.

"public" private courses

A step up in quality

A step above most municipal courses in quality and amenities are privately owned courses that are open to the public for a daily fee. Some of these courses let the public play year-round but give preference to their members when it comes to tee times and tournaments. Other private courses are open to the public only in the afternoon or in the "off" season, but again members get first dibs on tee times and other amenities.

Often, the price of admission—the greens fee—will give you a good idea of what kind of shape the course might be in. Courses with higher fees, for example, generally have smoother greens, better quality sand in the traps (yes, there is a difference, with some being clumpier than others), and lusher fairways. More expensive also generally means more difficult. Expensive courses can charge more than $75 for a round of golf and then up to another $30 for the use of a cart. Often they try to imitate the services offered at a private country club. Some give you free tees and dime-size plastic ball markers to use on the greens. They often have people to load and unload your clubs from your car.

Private golf courses often have fleets of golf carts available for rent.

ASK THE EXPERTS

Do I need to make reservations for a tee time?

If it's just you playing, you can usually get on without a reservation, especially if you want to play during the week and not the weekend. On weekend mornings, you'll have to wait until the **starter** (the person manning the reservation desk) finds three players who need one more to make a foursome. Singles are not usually allowed to play alone on weekends. If you have a foursome and want to play on the weekend, you may have to call and reserve a tee time. It's the same as at a popular restaurant. You call and say how many players you have in your party. Then you ask what times are available.

What if I don't want to use a golf cart?

There are some courses that require rental of a cart whether you want to use one or not. That's because the course gets the added revenue in fees for them. If you want to walk the course, ask whether it's possible before you go.

How do I know how difficult a course is?

Ask about its course rating and its slope (see page 50). An average course rating is 70 (the number of strokes it would take a pro to shoot par). An average slope rating is 113. Less than that means a fairly mild course. Close to 130 suggests a very difficult course. If you want to get familiar with a private course, see if its pro shop sells course guides or yardage books that describe holes and distances.

country club courses

Membership has its privileges

The golf and country club is an American institution. It's popular as a place where you not only have more say about the operation of the course but can also develop friendships that often transcend golf. Nearly all private clubs offer family memberships. Most provide swimming pools, tennis courts, and dining facilities.

Country clubs are known for their exclusivity—for a reason. They generally limit the number of memberships, usually 350 to 400 for an 18-hole course. This is to ensure a less crowded course at peak playing times. (Some private clubs are open to the public—see page 28—but members always have the first crack at tee times.) As a member, you also have access to practice areas as well as a pro shop and lessons from your club's pro.

Almost all private golf country clubs have a golf pro on hand. This pro is in charge of running the course, managing the pro shop (where you can buy golf equipment and apparel), and providing lessons. A good pro can make all the difference to the life and well-being of a country club. Before you join a club, meet with its pro and see what you think.

The bar or grill room of most golf clubs is often referred to as the 19th hole. Most private clubs also have larger, more formal dining rooms that serve breakfast, lunch, and dinner. Members are usually charged a monthly dining fee.

A Money Transaction

Joining a country club is not cheap. First there's the **initiation fee**, a one-time charge for joining, which you may or may not get back if you wish to leave the club. This fee can range from $1,000 to $100,000 and up. The average is around $20,000. This fee can be for "equity" or stock in the club. Like any stock, a membership's value can rise or fall with time. Note: If country club memberships are in high demand in your area, the initiation fee is sure to rise. Some clubs let you sell your membership, but charge a transfer fee, taking as much as a third of the  sale price to finance capital projects. Because the club deducts the amount from what you originally paid, you probably won't make money on the sale. At other clubs, the initiation fee is nonrefundable, nor can any of it be sold. These considerations should play into your calculations on whether a country club is worth the investment.

Once in, you'll be charged monthly dues—which can range from $150 to $500, depending on the club. Those dues cover your greens fees and cart fees. Most country clubs also have dining facilities. To make the facilities financially operable, members are usually charged a monthly dining fee, anywhere from $50 to $200. If the member eats at the club, the amount of the dinner is deducted from his monthly fee. If he doesn't eat there that month, he has to pay the fee anyway. Clearly, it pays to eat at the club.

If everything else fits, a country club is a good investment, especially if your whole family plays golf. Membership also provides ease of play and gives you instant eligibility to play in a club's many tournaments. Many country clubs offer reciprocal playing arrangements among clubs. Your club can arrange for you to play at various clubs in your town, around the country, or even overseas.

resort courses

The pampered golfer

If you're unable to join a private club but want to try your hand at a gorgeous golf course with all the amenities of a private club, consider going off to a golf resort. At the picturesque Coeur d'Alene resort in Idaho, the lodge and the course overlook a beautiful lake. You're taken from your resort hotel room to the course via an antique wooden boat. Once you're on the course, a forecaddie dressed in white coveralls discusses each hole with you while you follow in your cart. The bathrooms along the course are heated.

Many of the big resorts have spas, restaurants, tennis courts, swimming pools, and basketball courts, not to mention five or six different golf courses. Your day rate is based on which courses you play and the accommodations you pick. Golf resorts are located everywhere in the world.

ASK THE EXPERTS

I noticed there are a number of fine courses in a particular area. Is there any way I can stay at one resort and play these other courses?

Yes. There are areas around the U.S. where you simply pick out a hotel, and as part of your package you're allowed to play any of the golf courses nearby. Myrtle Beach is like that; so are Las Vegas, St. George in Utah, Phoenix, the Okanagan in British Columbia, and even Ireland and Scotland.

What should I look for in a resort golf course?

If you're a beginner, check to make sure the resort course is not too hard. Some resort courses are almost ridiculously difficult. Check the slope (see page 50). If it's over 125 from the white tees, you'd better be able to break 100 before you sign up. Some of the bigger resorts, like the Doral in Miami, offer a variety of courses, from the very difficult Blue Monster on down.

Where can I get information about resort golf courses?

The golf magazines (*Golf Digest* and *Golf Magazine*) often run features about various resort courses in the U.S. and around the world. The Zagat golf guide annually ranks and lists the top golf courses in the United States. You can also find information about golf resorts online by visiting **www.golfvacations.com**.

now what do I do?

Should I take lessons before I play on a real course?

Yes, yes, and yes. Trying to learn from a friend while you play your first game on a course is a hard way to break in. Your friend may know how to play but not how to teach you what you need to know. You need to know the proper grip and stance and swing. And you need to learn which clubs are used for which shots. That's a lot to learn your first time out.

How can I feel comfortable when I first play on a course?

Get in some practice first, on a driving range or with your instructor. Pick a course where you'll feel comfortable, preferably a good beginner's course like a 9-hole par-3 course. Have enough golf balls to cover you in case you lose a few. Six is usually plenty. Be ready to play when it's your turn. Have a basic understanding of the rules and etiquette of the game. Relax and keep a positive attitude, knowing that everyone around you started out this way and remembers what it was like to play a first round.

Should I walk or ride in a cart?

The game is less expensive and provides exercise even on a day when you aren't hitting the ball well if you walk. Get a light bag or a pull cart with wheels, which allows you to pull your cart along without too much effort—and walk.

Where can I go to take lessons?

Most courses have a professional, as do most driving ranges. Just ask at the counter of any pro shop at any golf course. There are private and group lessons. Clinics can be an easy and anonymous way to begin. They also cost less. You'll see others hitting as many bad shots as you are, and in some perverse way this can be comforting.

If tax dollars pay for municipal courses, why do I have to pay a fee?

Taxes cover some but not all of the costs of operating a golf course. Like national parks and other special public recreational facilities, users pay a fee to help offset the extra maintenance these places need. Golf courses need more attention than, for example, your local baseball field or neighborhood park, which you can usually use for free.

How can one of those hi-tech indoor driving ranges help me?

At these golf "studios," you hit balls into a net, and a computerized simulator measures how far the ball might have gone and in what direction it went. It also can tell you how many miles per hour you're swinging, and whether you hit the ball properly, with the face of the club square to the ball when the two met at impact. You'll see why your shots are going to the left (a hook or a pull) or to the right (a slice or a push). At some studios, you can practice hitting from different parts of the course, such as hitting shots out of sand traps or putting.

Helpful Resources

WEB SITES

www.USGA.org
This site offers good discussions of the rules and etiquette of golf

www.Legendinc.com
An interesting list of "The 10 Commandments of Golf Etiquette"

www.womensgolf.com
A site devoted to linking women golfers to pertinent sites

www.golfhelp.com
Comprehensive site discussing etiquette and rules

www.golflink.com
State-by-state guide to courses

www.privateclubmemberships.com
A site devoted to buying and selling memberships

golf.about.com/cs/travel/index.htm
Travel destinations for golfers

www.golfeurope.com
Comprehensive guide to golf clubs in Europe

www.worldgolf.com
A guide to golf destinations all over the world

BOOKS

Golf Rules Plain and Simple
by Mark Russell and John Andrisani

The Golfer's Code
by David Gould

Golf Is a Woman's Game
by Jane Horn

Golf Digest's Places to Play: The Latest Player Ratings of 6,000 Public and Resort Courses in the USA, Canada, Mexico, and the Islands
Published by Fodor's

Golf for Dummies
by Gary McCord

VIDEOS

Golf Tips by Sean Parees
Available from the author. Contact: sparees@quicksilvergolf.com

Chapter 3

The Golf Course

18-hole courses 38
How they work and why it's so hard

Par for the course 40
All about par 3s, 4s, and 5s

The tee 42
Where it all begins

The fairway 44
You're halfway there

Hazards 46
When your ball lands on sand or in water

The putting green 48
Where you can really improve your score

Course ratings 50
Why each golf course is unique

Now what do I do? 52
Answers to common questions

HOW A PRO
WOULD PLAY IT

Difficult par 3
246 yards

"For this long par 3, I'd hit my tee
shot to the center of the green."

18-hole courses

The average golf course has 18 holes. This means your typical course is about four miles long. Most courses consist of

- four par-5 holes
- ten par-4 holes
- four par-3 holes

But golf course architects have put more thought into the process than just creating holes with various pars. Most golf holes are strategic. For your ability, there's a best way to play the hole. Often it's a matter of risk and reward. If you can, try to visualize the hole backward. Ask yourself, what is the best place to take a shot to get to the green? To get to that position you might need to take your tee shot over a fairway bunker. Can you do that? Or should you play safe and take a less efficient—but also less dangerous—route? Whatever you do, don't forget to factor in that tiny little creek on the left or the tall clump of trees on the right. Thanks to the diabolical mind of the architect, the possibilities are endless, as are the challenges.

The Art of Golf Course Design

The design of golf courses has a lot to do with the size and type of land available. A course in Florida is going to be different from one in Scotland. The original golf course designers, like Old Tom Morris and Alister Mackenzie, didn't have great earth-moving equipment, so they worked with what they had. Their courses followed the rugged terrain of the land in Scotland and Ireland. Two American golf designers, Robert Trent Jones, Sr., and Pete Dye, have done much to transform the game from its rugged Highland roots. Their courses are noted for their beauty and ingenious use of hazards.

As wonderful stretches of rolling land become more expensive, golf course architects today are inserting more man-made obstacles, creating so-called target golf, with the need to play from one area to another by successfully hitting the ball across water or large amounts of sand. Each area of the country has its own special obstacles to contend with—tall trees in the north, strong wind on the coasts, sand and cactus in the Southwest, and swampy waterways in the Southeast.

Opposite page: An aerial view of one of the two 18-hole courses at the Baltusrol Golf Club in Springfield, New Jersey. The dual courses were designed and built by the renowned architect Albert W. Tillinghast, who was one of the first to articulate and apply the principles of modern golf course design.

par for the course

Different strokes

The old golf phrase "par for the course" suggests that par is what we ought to make on each hole. Well, it isn't. Par is what an expert golfer is expected to record on a hole without making any mistakes. There are only three types of par: par 3, par 4, and par 5. The USGA, the governing body of golf in the U.S., establishes the yardage range for those pars. When you add up the pars on an 18-hole course, it should come to 70, 71, or 72 par for the course.

As a beginner, you shouldn't think for a moment about the usual 72 par for the course. Instead, you should focus on something called your **personal par**—in other words, shooting your personal handicap or better. If you haven't established a handicap yet, your first goal should be to have no more than two strokes over par per hole. This is called a **double bogey**. Do that consistently over 18 holes and you'll shoot a 108. Once you've accomplished that, go for shooting one over par. This is called a **bogey** and adds up to a total score of 90. On many courses, a bogey can be a very good score.

At the beginning of each hole you will find a hole marker that tells you the distance from the various tee markers. Here the distance from the championship tee (the farthest from the green) is 188 yards; it's 100 yards from the junior's tee, which is closest to the green.

ASK THE EXPERTS

What determines the par on a hole?

For the most part, its length, or the number of yards from tee to green. Par 3s range from 100 yards to 250 yards, par 4s from 260 to 460, and par 5s from 460 to 600. Each hole allows for two putts on the green. So to make par on a par 3, it's assumed you would hit your tee shot onto the green and take two putts for a 3. A par 4 allows for a drive down the fairway, an approach to the green, and two putts. A par 5 is what is called a three-shot hole with a drive, a second shot to within 100 yards or so of the hole, a third shot onto the green, and two putts.

Are par 5s the toughest holes?

They're the longest, but not the toughest. In fact, the par 5 often gives an average player the best chance at making par. Let's say the hole is 480 yards, and after a 200-yard drive and a 180-yard second shot the player is left with a 100-yard shot to the green. That's much easier than a 180-yard second shot to the green, which can be the norm on a par 4, or a 180-yard tee shot on a par 3. Some golfers who hit the ball a long way can reach the par 5 in two shots, making it possible to finish out with just two putts.

What's a birdie and what's an eagle?

In golf, these words have nothing to do with winged fowl. A birdie is one shot under par. So if you are playing on a par-5 hole and shoot a four, you are one under par. That's great! If you shoot two under par on a hole, that's an eagle. And that's really terrific!

the tee

Where the hole begins

You hit your first shot for the hole from the **tee**, a level lawnlike grass area. This area is marked with several different-colored large plastic balls or square plastic blocks on either side. You're supposed to place your ball anywhere you want between two similar-colored large balls. But you don't just drop the ball on the ground. For this important shot, you tee it up. To do that you use a **tee,** a three-inch wooden or plastic ball holder that is inserted into the ground. You then place your ball on top of the tee, making your tee shot easier to hit than if it were simply lying on the ground.

Which of the large plastic balls do you use when lining up your tee shot? Naturally, being golf, there is a tee system to help level the playing field. On most golf courses, there are three to four different tee markers on each hole, and these markers all have different colors to indicate where each category of golfers should tee off from. The standard color code is as follows: Black tee marker balls for pros, blue or white for men; red for women; yellow for juniors and seniors.

Some players will say they want to "play it the way the pros do" by playing from the tees that make the course the longest. Stay away from those tees. Put your ego in your pocket. Use your brains instead. The game is so much more enjoyable if played from the right tees. For the male golfer with a handicap from 10 to 30, that means using the white tees. Women generally play red tees.

Playing from the right tees means you'll play the course as it was designed. The bunkers in the fairways will come into play on your drive, just as they will for the pros teeing off way back on the black tees. Find the tees that make the game most enjoyable for you, and don't be talked into something different.

Use your hand and gently push the wooden tee into the ground. Try to consistently set the tee at the same height.

Strategies at Tee Time

When you're on the tee, you put your ball on a wooden prop, also known as a **tee**. Teeing up at the start of each hole is one of the few assists you're given in golf. Take advantage of it. Be careful when placing your tee in the ground that you don't get ahead of the tee markers. You can go behind the markers as long as you aren't farther back than the length of two clubs. This rectangle defines the tee block. Most golfers favor the front of the box.

Where should you put your ball? That depends on what lies ahead of you. Say there's a lake on the right side of the fairway. Some pros suggest that you tee up on the side of trouble. By putting your tee in the ground nearer to the right tee block, you're more able to direct your shot safely to the left. The opposite works if the hazard is on the left. Tee up on the left, aiming to the right.

The handicap system allows players to use different tees. But once you pick your tee marker color, you must stick to it for the rest of the game. No switching from blue to white. If your playing partners want to play from a more difficult set of tees, you don't have to play off theirs. Stay with the tee that's right for you.

The tee markers are color coded and usually follow this pattern:

Blue or black:
"Back tee" (men's)

White:
"Middle tee" (forward men's tee)

Red:
"Forward tee" (women's tee)

Yellow:
Juniors' and seniors' tee

Tee Markers

the fairway

Adventures on a course's fringe

Those beautiful trees that line many golf course holes are there for a reason. They define the hole and defend par, like soldiers lined up in a row. Your goal is to hit the ball onto the closely mowed grass, called the **fairway**. This grass is usually smooth and cut fairly low. On the sides of the fairway lies the **rough**, or longer grass, often cut in degrees of difficulty as it gets farther from the fairway.

Trees near greens have several purposes: They protect the shorter grass from burning out in the sun, they help frame the hole so you can see it from a distance, and they serve as a hazard for errant shots.

Hitting your ball into the rough will happen a lot when you start learning the game. As you get better, you'll learn to stay clear of it. When you land in the rough, don't assume the grass is like the fairway grass. Because the grass is longer, it's going to grab your club and make it difficult to hit the ball very far. Use a club with more **loft** (having a head that's less perpendicular to the ground), like a wedge or a 9-iron to better extract the ball (for more on clubs, see pages 78–85). First and foremost you want to get the ball back on the short grass.

Rules of the Rough

Rough is, well, rough. If you land in it, check the rule book. Typically, you're allowed five minutes to hunt for your ball. If you're lucky enough to find it, all you can do according to the rule book (see page 59 for more on rules) is take a peek at it to see how deeply buried it really is. You can't move the ball; you can, however, remove sticks and leaves that are covering your ball or in the way of your golf stroke.

Beginners sometimes just pick up their ball and put it in the fairway to give themselves a better chance to hit a good shot and speed up play. That's not necessarily a bad instinct, but it's not legal. You'll know you're no longer a beginner when you take your medicine for hitting a bad shot and hack the ball out onto the fairway.

hazards

On the beach or taking a drink

Remember trying to avoid jail when you played Monopoly? Hazards should be looked at the same way when playing golf. Hazards, such as a lake at the edge of a fairway or a **bunker** (sand trap) surrounding a green, aren't accidental. They're intentional design elements of a golf course, to spice up the game.

Even the pros fall prey to bunkers—that's why it's important to practice sand shots.

Water hazards, in particular, are a curse to some players. These little rivers or small lakes are usually marked with red or yellow stakes to signal to hapless golfers that they're in dangerous territory. If your ball lands in the water and you can fish it out, you still must take a penalty stroke. If you can't find your ball, you also must take a penalty stroke. Either way, you must play a new or newly dripping ball close to where it entered the water hazard.

Mercifully, there is no penalty for being in a bunker or sand trap except the difficulty of trying to hit the ball out. That's because you're not allowed to put your club on the sand as you prepare to hit the shot. Very tricky. Also, etiquette stipulates that after you hit your shot, you need to smooth the sand with a rake that will usually be lying nearby. This will leave the bunker nice and playable for the next victim.

ASK THE EXPERTS

What are the differences between the red and yellow stakes?

A pond sitting in front of a green, for example, is defined by **yellow stakes.** If you go in the water, you mark where your ball last crossed the line surrounding the hazard. From there you can go back from the hazard as far as you want, as long as you keep your point of entry into the hazard between you and the hole. You incur a one-stroke penalty. **Red stakes** define a lateral hazard, meaning the water runs alongside the hole. Since you can't go back to take your next shot, you're allowed to drop the ball two club-lengths on either side of the hazard. And add a stroke, of course.

What if there's no water in the water hazard?

Occasionally that happens. A pond or a creek dries up. The area should still be marked by red or yellow stakes. If you fall within the marked areas, then you are in the hazard, water or not. You can always play the ball out of the hazard without penalty, but remember, you can't put your club on the ground before hitting the shot.

To spice up the game, golf designers often add water hazards around the green.

the putting green

Drive for show,
putt for dough

Putting doesn't involve size or strength or even much athletic ability. Yet it is terribly important. As they say, a three-foot putt counts the same as a 300-yard drive. Unlike the past when greens were slow and bumpy, today's putting surface is usually smooth, and it's possible to sink a putt with just one stroke.

Putting greens are typically about 5,000 square feet in size. Somewhere in there stands a flagstick, which marks the coveted spot: the cup. Most putting greens are irregular in shape and size on purpose. Nearly all have some kind of slope to them. This means that after you hit your ball with your putter, your ball will turn, or **break**, left or right as it encounters a slope placed perilously near the cup. (Those golf course designers are keen on making golf challenging.)

Once you get used to putting, you'll learn how to "read the green," which means seeing how much break there might be. Once you figure that out, you can better determine the line the putt should follow and then decide how fast the ball needs to travel.

The pros only make 50 percent of their putts from five feet, and probably only 20 percent from 15 feet or more. It's not so important that you make long putts but that you get the first putt close enough to the hole so you can make the second one.

Some people find that they can better read the break by using their putter as a plumb line. Hold the putter with one hand near the top, and gravity will make the putter drop to a true 90-degree angle.

Get in the Zone

Often golfers will complain that while they played a great game, they just couldn't sink a putt, not even the short ones. And the more putts they missed, the worse their putting became. That's because the number one reason for poor putting is anxiety about making a putt. To combat that, try to keep your mind free of any expectations. Just focus on your stroke. Keep your shoulders loose and your arms straight. To take their minds off their anxiety, some golfers hum when they putt.

Try to keep your nose directly over the putter and don't move anything but your shoulders during the swing.

FIRST PERSON DISASTER STORY

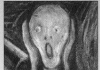

Miniature golf it's not

As a kid, I had always been an ace miniature golfer. When I finally got around to taking up the game of golf as a grown woman, I was certain that putting would be the least of my problems. Was I wrong! I had learned all kinds of bad habits on the miniature golf course, like using a different stance if the hole warranted it. I finally realized I needed a lesson in putting. What a difference. It turns out it was my hand-eye coordination that helped me win at miniature golf, not my putting stroke.

—Mary T., Seattle, Washington

course ratings

You against the course

For an inanimate object, a golf course plays a particularly tough form of defense. While it's true that no defender will jump in front of you, bent on blocking your shot, the golf course you're playing on will throw up plenty of challenges. The more challenging the course, the higher its rating. An easy course is rated 66 or 67, which is how many strokes a pro would need for 18 holes. A course with a 72 rating means a pro should take no more than 72 shots.

Sand shots over water make a course more difficult.

What goes into a course's rating? First there is the sheer length of the course to consider. Most courses are around 6,500 yards long. The longer the course, the higher its rating.

As if length isn't enough, most courses have built-in challenges to conquer. There are trees to avoid. And then there are bunkers (natural or man-made wonders strategically placed on a hole and filled with sand or thick grass). Getting out of a bunker is tough; most new golfers need to take several strokes to get back to the sweet, short grass of the fairway. Finally, there are water hazards (creeks or ponds that seem to be right in the way of where you want to go). Land in a water hazard and you not only lose your ball, but you also get a penalty stroke, which adds a stroke to your score. Ouch.

All those challenges or obstacles are combined to give a course its **slope**. The slope takes into account how narrow the course is as well as how many water hazards and bunkers it has. An average slope rating is 113. Less than that means a fairly mild course. A number near 130 suggests a very difficult course. In fact, each hole on a course is rated for its difficulty—the easiest hole is rated 18, the hardest is given a 1 rating. The ratings of all the holes are combined to create the course slope. You should see these ratings listed on the golf course scorecards.

ASK THE EXPERTS

Who rates the golf courses?

The USGA authorizes and trains state and regional golf associations across the country to measure and rate the golf courses in their states.

What strokes do you have to count?

All of them. If you swing at the ball with intent to hit it, you count the stroke even if you miss the ball. That can be hard on beginners. Beginners often move the ball from deep grass to a place from which they're more likely to hit a good shot; just know that the rules of golf say you play the ball as it lies except when permitted to lift the ball by a rule.

What if I hit the ball over a fence or into the water?

Hitting it over a fence, you'll probably have to add a penalty stroke to your total. If you hit the ball off the course (known as out of bounds), you have to take a stroke penalty and hit the ball again from where you originally did. You count the original stroke, the penalty stroke, and then the stroke to hit the shot all over again. Instead of "lying one" after your drive, you are now "lying three." A shot in the water incurs a penalty shot as well, although you can usually hit your next shot from close to where the ball entered the water in addition to where it was originally struck.

now what do I do?

How should I dress for the golf course?

Most golf courses require that men wear a collared shirt, which means no T-shirts. Cutoffs and short-shorts are often frowned upon, as are tank tops for women and men. Many courses won't allow jeans. Sneakers are generally okay. Golf shoes should probably have soft spikes instead of the old metal spikes.

What equipment is necessary before heading to the course?

Golf courses require that each player have a set of clubs. You'll need at least a half dozen golf balls. You'll lose a few, but being out in the woods so much means you'll also find a few. You'll need tees (you can buy a package in the pro shop for less than a dollar) and something with which to mark your ball's location on the green—a thin coin does nicely. There are small tools available at pro shops to repair the indentation on a green that an incoming shot can make. If you don't have one, you can use a tee.

Do beginners really need to play by the rules?

Good question, hard answer. They need to understand the spirit of the rules: that you count every shot, that you play the ball as it lies, and that you are penalized for going out of bounds and in hazards. Sometimes it's prudent to drop a ball near where your shot went out of bounds instead of going back to the tee to hit the shot again, as per the rules. The better decision is to play a provisional ball when you think you're out of bounds or your ball might be lost. That saves having to go back and hit again, which saves time, an important consideration on the course. In the beginning, you'll improve a lie here and there (see page 58 for more about improving lies). But after a while, you won't, because you'll understand just how important the rules are.

Does a course always start with a par 4?

The typical course will have four par 5s, four par 3s, and ten par 4s. But that can vary. Some new courses are designed with six par 5s, six par 3s, and six par 4s, much to the delight of the average player, who seems to have a better chance of making a par on a par 5 than on the others. While a par 4 is the normal opening hole, many courses start with a par 5, and a few with a par 3.

What's the best way to keep from slowing down play?

To move along and get the round over with in a decent time for you and all those playing behind you, you need to be ready to hit when it's your turn. If you want to study the greens the way Tiger Woods does, then do it while others are putting and not when it's your turn to putt. The same can be said for taking practice swings. Do it while others are hitting, but away from their line of sight. Then when it's your turn, fire away. Socialize while you're walking between shots, not on the greens or the tee boxes. If you want to impress your playing companions, play quickly. They care more about how fast you play than how well you play. If you are keeping everyone waiting, pick up your ball and move on.

Beginning golfers should follow the rule of 10. If you have hit more than 10 shots on one hole, then stop playing and pick up your ball and start fresh on the next hole. Hitting more than 10 shots on a hole is not only frustrating, but a waste of time and energy. It's best to stop and start anew on the next hole.

Helpful Resources

WEB SITES

www.golfhelp.com
A site designed to help with etiquette and rules

BOOKS

Golf Rules Explained
by Peter Dobereiner

Nicklaus by Design: Golf Course Strategy and Architecture
by Jack Nicklaus

Chapter 4

On the Course

The rule book 56
Lots of things to know

When problems arise 58
What the rule book says

Course etiquette 60
The unwritten rules of golf

Respecting the course 62
Replacing divots, raking bunkers

The golf cart 64
Taking everything with you

Walking the course 66
Being your own caddie

Types of local matches 68
Best ball, foursome, scramble, Nassau

Country club tournaments 70
Member-Member, Couples golf

Playing it safe 72
How to prevent injuries

Now what do I do? 74
Answers to common problems

HOW A PRO
WOULD PLAY IT

Difficult par 4
458 yards

"This is a very tough hole with hazards on both sides of a narrow fairway. I'd try to drive my tee-off to the right. On my second shot I'd use a 6-iron to the green; a long iron may bounce your shot into one of the traps."

the rule book

Know the rules before you start playing

Like any other game, golf has rules that players must follow. The USGA is the keeper of the definitive rule book, which is called simply *The Rules of Golf*. This little book contains all 34 rules and their definitions, which apply whenever the game is played. There is no distinction in the rules between professional and amateur golfers—the rules are applied uniformly.

The rules explain the two basic forms of golf: stroke play and matchplay. **Stroke play** is when a group of players play a specified number of holes and the player with the lowest total number of strokes is the winner. Most tournaments at the professional level are played using this format. **Matchplay** is historically the older form of play and pits one golfer or one team against another golfer or team on a hole-by-hole basis, with each hole worth one point. It does not matter how many strokes you take to win the hole. In matchplay you can either win, lose, or halve a hole. The winner is the player or team that is leading by a number of holes greater than the number of holes remaining to be played.

The Rules of Golf

And the Rules of Amateur Status

2002 - 2003

When you join the USGA, you will get a copy of *The Rules of Golf.* Hard-core golfers can purchase its *Decisions on the Rules of Golf,* which describes the rulings for every conceivable problem a golfer might encounter.

ASK THE EXPERTS

Why are there so many rules in golf?

As the rule book explains, golf is unique among sports in that it is not played on a defined playing area as are tennis and football. Golf is played on courses with differing terrains and varying weather conditions, not to mention the occasional encounters with indigenous wildlife. The rules were created to try to cover as many of these situations as possible so all golfers would know what to do. Like the rules of driving that apply around the world, golfing rules let golfers all over the globe know what is right and wrong.

Where can I get a copy of *The Rules of Golf* book?

The Rules of Golf may be purchased online for $1.00 per copy plus shipping and handling at **www.usgapubs.com**, or call the USGA Order Department toll-free at 1-800-336-4446, Monday through Friday 9 am–5 pm (EST). For additional information on *The Rules of Golf* and an online version of the book, visit **www.rulesofgolf.com** on the Internet. If you join the USGA, they will send you a rule book along with some other goodies.

My sister is a member of a country club and they have their own "rule" book. What is that about?

Most courses have their own book with various club policies. These policies cover all sorts of things particular to that club; for instance, the use of cell phones, their dress code, and their fees for guests. It usually lists the dates of various golf tournaments throughout the year, and hours of play for men, women, and junior golfers. Most clubs also have "local rules" that address specific situations that may be encountered while playing their courses. These local rules can supplement the official rules of golf but not waive or modify them.

when problems arise

Let the rules help you out

The rules of golf are based on two fundamental principles: Play the ball as it lies, and play the course as you find it. The old Scottish golfers who invented the game had a thing about these principles—they felt they kept everyone honest. And they do.

But because golf is played outside in all different kinds of seasons, on varying courses, golf's rule book covers many varied situations. The rules provide **relief** from some of the situations encountered. For example, if your ball comes to rest on a sprinkler head or cart path in the fairway or rough, you may take relief without penalty.

Naturally, there will be times when the relief available comes with a cost, a **penalty** stroke, such as when you do not wish to play your ball from within a water hazard!

After you have played from within a bunker, you are responsible for raking out your footprints and any other damage you have made in the bunker.

When Things Aren't Perfect

Lost Ball or **Out of Bounds**. If you've hit a wild shot and think your ball might be lost outside a water hazard or out of bounds, you have two options. One is to take a penalty stroke, and tee off again with a new ball, thus hitting your third shot. Another option is to tee off again with another ball declaring it a "provisional ball." Once you get to the area where you think you lost your first ball, you can hunt for it for five minutes. If you find it, you can play it and pick up your provisional ball. If you don't find your first ball, you take a penalty stroke and continue to play the hole with your provisional ball.

Preferred Lies/Winter Rules. Some clubs allow for something called either preferred lies or winter rules. That's when the course is in such an unusual condition (often because of extreme weather) that those in charge of the course believe that, in order to ensure fair play, a local rule should be adopted permitting a player to "prefer" his or her lie. This rule allows the player to pick up the ball, clean it, and place it within a specified distance from its original location.

course etiquette

The links include their own rules

Whether you're practicing on a golf range or playing on an 18-hole course, golf is half skill and half fitting in. Fitting in is about learning the unwritten rules, like what shoes to wear—sneakers are fine if you don't have golf shoes. Or what to do if your swing knocks out a clump of grass, known as a **divot**. The answer is retrieve it and put it back so that the ground is flat should another player's ball land on that exact same spot.

Over time, you will pick up on golf's customs. You'll learn more about course etiquette on page 172, but here are some golf guidelines:

■ Wait quietly while your opponents are hitting to give them their best chance to succeed.

■ Keep at a distance so you stay out of the way of another golfer's swing.

■ Avoid standing directly behind the player hitting, or within his or her peripheral vision. Stand along the side, facing the player's chest or back.

■ Compliment a good shot even though it may put you behind in a competition. Don't cheer a bad shot even though it may put you ahead.

■ Keep the game moving by going to the next shot as soon as you can.

■ Putting does not begin until all the balls are on the green. Then the player with the ball farthest from the pin putts first.

■ The honor of teeing off first is given to the player who has the lowest score on the previous hole.

ASK THE EXPERTS

What do I wear?

You probably have something to wear already—a shirt with a collar and a pair of khaki pants or shorts. Sneakers are fine to start, but as you get into the game, you'll find golf shoes with their rubber cleats provide a better grip when you're swinging a club in soft grass. Women can wear pants or shorts or skirts (shorts and shirts should not be too short). Leave your tank tops, short-shorts, and cutoff jeans behind. Get a golf glove to protect your hand.

How do I know who tees off first on the first hole?

You can decide among yourselves. Otherwise, you can flip a tee among four players to find out which one has honors—or the right to go first. Whoever the tip of the tee points to goes first. After the initial tee shot, the person whose ball is farthest from the green (the area around the cup) is considered to be away and traditionally shoots first. On each successive hole, the player with the best score on the preceding hole wins honors and gets to tee off first.

How fast should I play?

Pace yourself so that a round of 18 holes takes about three to four hours. Feel free to take a practice swing, but skip taking many more so that the game keeps moving. (Only the professionals on TV get to take their time before they take a shot.)

respecting the course

Replacing divots, raking bunkers

Like hiking in a national park or picnicking at a beach, you should leave the course in better condition than you found it. Of course that means leaving no cans or sandwich wrappers. But it also means repairing any damage you do to the course. It's easy to accidentally tear up the course or to make footprints that might send someone else's ball astray. It's even easier to fix it. Replace the chunk of grass (called a **divot**) you or any other player might have unearthed.

Keep in mind that those who've played the course before you have done likewise. They've made it easier for you to play. Do the same for those who follow you.

Most courses make it easy for you. On the tees, you can often find buckets of sand and grass seed that you can use to fill any gouges you made with your tee-off swing. If you wind up in a bunker (a hazard with sand), rake the sand before you leave. And if your ball leaves a dent or other mark on the green, dig around the dent with a tee to raise the earth above the level of the green, then use your putter to tap the earth back down so it is now flat. Also on the green, steer clear of leaving footmarks in the putting path of any of your playing companions.

You sometimes need to take a divot to get under a ball when using a short iron. Digging into the grass under the ball allows you to get backspin on the ball so it will stop when it lands on the green. Remember, you must replace any divot you make.

ASK THE EXPERTS

Who grabs the flagstick?

At the end of each hole is the green with its coveted little metal cup, which is guarded by a flagstick. The player whose ball is nearest the cup usually "tends" the flagstick, also known as the pin. The flagstick must not be in the cup while someone is putting on the green in case a ball hits the stick and bounces out down the green. (You can only leave the flag in if you are putting from the fringe.) If you are playing with a caddie—someone who carries your clubs—then the caddie tends the flagstick.

Why do pros "mark" the ball on the green?

You are not allowed to touch the ball until it is on the green. At that point you can mark it by placing a round coin or marker directly behind the ball to indicate its position. Marking the ball allows you to pick it up and clean off grass, dirt, or sand. It also allows you to move your ball out of another's way. In putting, those furthest away from the pin putt first. When it is your turn to putt, you replace the ball directly in front of your marker.

The golf cart

Why walk when you can ride?

Almost any course you might play will rent you a golf cart. These gas or electrically powered carts carry two people and two sets of clubs. They are easy to operate. You just turn the key, push a lever near the seat bottom to "forward," and press down the accelerator like you would in a car. There is also a brake that can be locked when you stop, by pushing it all the way down. Upon taking off, be sure your clubs are strapped securely on the back. You don't want them falling off as you near the first tee. There is also room in the cart to hold cold drinks and some snacks.

For inclement weather, some carts include side curtains to enclose the open-air cabin. The plastic sides keep out rain. Figure that use of a cart will add $12 to $40 to your round, depending on whether you share the cart with someone else or take it out by yourself.

Sometimes you won't have a choice about whether you take a cart or walk and carry or pull your clubs. Some courses are so hilly and the holes so far apart from each other that course regulations demand you use a cart. In that case, the charge will be included in your greens fees.

FIRST PERSON DISASTER STORY

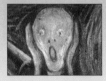

Buckle Up

It was one of those fancy corporate outings, you know, where you want to impress everybody with how together you are on the course. I was set to tee off first on the first tee. I hit a decent tee shot, but as we left to head down the first fairway, my clubs fell off the cart. I'd put my golf bag on the cart but forgotten to strap it in adequately. Everyone got a good laugh, except me. Next time, I'll pay attention to the finer details of the game.

Wilson M., Naples, Florida

Fairway Driving

In summer, you can drive a golf cart almost everywhere on a course except near the greens. Just look for the small signs near greens that indicate "no carts." In winter, carts are often limited to the cart paths. This means you have to park on the path and walk to your ball. Make sure to carry a number of clubs because you won't know exactly what you need until you get there. Occasionally, you are permitted to drive from the cart path directly to the ball at a 90-degree angle, thus the proviso the "90-degree rule for golf carts today."

Some golf communities allow you to use your own golf cart on and off the course.

walking the course

A fine walk in the open air

If at all possible, try walking a course. You can count the benefits:

1. The round costs less.

2. You get exercise.

3. You spend more quiet time talking to your companions as you get closer to the putting green.

4. Walking keeps your muscles in motion, so your swing will be loose.

5. You get a better feel for the hole and a good sense of how the architect designed it.

Technology has made clubs and bags lighter. The new generation of bags that is designed to be carried has a set of legs that pop open to keep the bag upright when you set it down. The legs keep the bag and your clubs out of the mud or wet grass and also keep you from having to bend over to repeatedly pick up the clubs.

Alternatively, you can use a **pull cart**—a wheeled contraption that rolls your bag along the ground as you pull or push the cart's handle. Today's pull carts are made of light metals and have big wheels that make them easy to use.

A low-tech item goes high tech: Pull carts now come battery-powered. Flip the switch and watch it move on its own. This model can be directed to your ball by remote control.

ASK THE EXPERTS

How do I find out whether I can walk the course rather than ride in a cart?

Most municipal courses will let you walk. For other types of courses, you'll need to call and ask. Expect that in an organized tournament you will have to use a golf cart to keep the game moving quickly.

Does the round take less time if you use a cart?

Yes, if carts are permitted on the fairways, and the course is laid out around a housing community. If the carts are restricted to the cart paths, then walking may be faster because of the extra time required for a cart driver to get to each shot.

In terms of exercise, if I carry my clubs, how far will I walk?

In a straight line, not counting distance between greens and the next tee, you will cover about four miles. But then, what golfer ever hit all the balls in a straight line? Figure about five miles total. That's great exercise. If you carry your clubs, you add strengthening to your routine.

Pull carts are now made of lightweight metals and have other features that make them easier to handle and use.

types of local matches

Scrambling your way to success

After a few lessons, some time at the driving range, and some rounds on the course, you might really enjoy a local tournament.

Enter the world of matchplay. Unlike the straight stroke game where the player with the lowest score wins, in tournaments the winner is usually the one with the greatest number of low-scoring holes. For starters, consider the **scramble.** Here you'll be assigned to a **foursome**—a group of four golf players. As a group, you each tee off and then play the best shot among the four players. This puts less pressure on you to play great. One good shot—say, a putt—can help your team. It's a great way to chat, joke about one another's shots, and get some tips. In a **best-ball** tournament, again less pressure is put on you to play well. You count your score on each hole, but you can forget a bad hole if your partner has had a good one. Only one score between the two of you counts on each hole.

You might have heard the term **Nassau**—a very popular way to jazz up your golf game. Here, you get a point for winning the first nine holes, the second nine, and then for all 18 holes. A $2 Nassau means you can win as much as $6 by winning the front nine, the back nine, and the 18. It also means you can lose as much as $6.

Betting and Golf

Betting is a constant in golf. The extra competition it introduces seems to sharpen your concentration and keep you involved in what you are doing. Of course, only bet what you can afford, and don't be afraid to turn down an offer to bet if it's not your cup of tea.

The bets people make are endless in nature. Golfers have come up with their own weird and wacky bets. You can get a point for hitting a tree and still making a par—this is called a barkie. A sandie is making par after you've been in a sand trap. Have fun.

Once the round is over, it is customary to gather afterward to celebrate the round, pay off bets, and plan the next time you can be together. It's a good idea for winners of the competition to use a portion of their winnings to buy soft drinks or sandwiches for the losers.

country club tournaments

Scrambling your way to success

There are several standard tournaments that most private country clubs offer, namely the **Club-Championship, Member-Member, Member-Guest**, and **Couples**. The Club Championship is held for the coveted title of club champion. This tournament is played much like the professionals' tournaments. The player with the lowest total score wins. Usually a plaque with the winner's name is hung in a place of honor in the clubhouse. Most clubs have a men's championship tournament as well as a women's championship tournament. These are usually played in handicap flights (or divisions) so all players can compete.

The Member-Member is a tournament where two members team up to play against another member twosome. In the Member-Guest, a club member invites a guest to play in a twosome against other Member-Guest twosomes. In both the Member-Member and Member-Guest, the tournament can be based on the total lowest team score or it can be a best ball or even a scramble, depending on what the club members decide. Couples matches pit mixed couples (typically husband and wife) against other couples. The twosome can play best ball or a scramble.

There are lots of other matches throughout the year. There are front-nine contests (played on the first nine holes) as well as back-nine contests (on the last nine holes), not to mention tournaments for junior golfers.

Couples and Tournaments

Dating someone who plays golf? You might want to look into playing **Scotch Ball**. The couple uses one ball, alternates hitting shots, and tests their games as well as their relationship.

Just don't get suckered into gender issues about playing from "men's" or "women's" tees. You should each tee off from the tees that best suit you. If you're both starting off, each of you may prefer the red tees, formerly referred to as the "women's" tees. These days, courses are no longer calling them men's and women's tees, but back, middle, and forward tees.

playing it safe

Avoiding trouble

Golf is a gentle sport compared to soccer or football. It provides good overall muscular conditioning and, if you walk the course, a nice easy workout. But like any activity, a little brain before brawn goes a long way toward preventing unnecessary injuries. For instance, golf clubs are heavy. Don't wrench your back by reaching way back into your car trunk to lift out your clubs. Have someone help you pull them out. (And be sure to lift from your legs, not your back.)

Warming up before you play is always smart. Do some stretching exercises in the locker room or near the first tee. To stretch your back and side muscles, put a club across your neck or back; now rotate your torso. Next try holding two clubs in one hand and swinging them together, starting easily with short swings and then increasing into a full swing.

Before you get on the course, apply sunscreen. Wear a golf hat or a baseball hat, and always use a glove. Be sure to drink plenty of water. Most courses have water fountains at the 9th hole, but carry a bottle of water if you can. Get proper sleep before you play, and don't miss breakfast because your tee time is too early. It is a good idea to pack some snacks if you are playing in a tournament. Avoid noisy, crunchy food or snacks that leave crumbs everywhere. A hard-boiled egg is good, as is a banana.

ASK THE EXPERTS

What do I do if there is a storm with thunder and lightning while I am playing?

Take cover as quickly as possible. Avoid trees and other tall objects, which are more likely to be hit by lightning. If there is no shelter to be found, then leave your clubs by the rough and sit or lie down in the fairway until the storm passes.

I am allergic to bee stings. Are golf courses safe to play?

The odds of getting stung on your local golf course are no greater than the odds of getting stung while taking a walk in your neighborhood, the only difference being the difficulty in getting medical treatment if you get stung on the course. For that reason, if you have a severe bee allergy, you need to carry medications with you to combat an allergic reaction should you get stung. Alert your team players to your allergy. Note: Bees are attracted to sugary substances. Don't drink out of a soda can while playing; bees have been known to get inside the cans without players noticing.

Is it possible to get hit by a golf ball?

It's a rare occurrence, but it does happen. That's why golfers yell "fore" to warn unsuspecting players to take cover from a wayward ball. If you do get hit, stop playing and seek first aid.

Golf First Aid Kit

Most seasoned players have a little homemade first aid kit tucked away in their golf bag. It doesn't have to be a big deal; just a few essentials are good to have on hand:

Sunscreen
Insect repellent
Allergy medicine

Band-Aids
Aspirin or Ibuprophen
Tissues

now what do I do?

Do women golfers have their own club tournaments?

Yes, they do. Most country clubs have separate men's and women's golf committees. They run their own tournaments, such as the Ladies Member-Member or the Ladies Member-Guest.

Are there separate areas in a club for women and men?

The only really "separate" areas are the Ladies Locker Room and the Men's Locker Room. These are the rooms where golfers can shower and change their clothes. Alas, some women members are still not allowed into certain dining areas in exclusive clubs. Worse, some private country clubs still do not allow women to become members.

What is a dog-leg?

To make the game interesting and challenging, golf course designers try to make each hole intriguing. A dog-leg is golf slang for a hole that has a fairly severe turn to it. If the hole turns to the right, it's called a "dog-leg to the right"; if it's to the left, then it's a "dog-leg to the left."

What is fore and why do golfers yell it out?

Fore is golfing shorthand for "danger, look out!" Golfers yell it when they hit a wild shot and it may come within striking distance of another player. When you hear "fore" cover your head with your arms.

Can women play any time at all clubs?

Some clubs restrict times women can play.

What is a good score?

Ninety percent of golfers shoot over 100. Your goal is always to compete against yourself and try to improve your game stroke by stroke.

What is "sudden death"?

When pros play in the professional tournaments, they are playing stroke play. The scores for each hole are totaled to give a gross score. No handicap is used. If there is a tie for first place, then the tournament goes into "sudden death." This means the tied players now must compete on a hole-by-hole basis. If there is no winner on the first hole, then a second hole is played and so on, until one player scores less on the hole than the others. That player is the winner.

What are preferred lies/winter rules?

Some golf courses allow for something called either preferred lies or winter rules. That's when the course is in such an unusual condition (often because of extreme weather) that those in charge of the course believe that, in order to ensure fair play, a local rule should be adopted permitting a player to "prefer" his or her lie. This allows the player to pick up the ball, clean it, and place it within a specified distance from its original location.

Helpful Resources

WEB SITES

www.USGA.org
This site offers good discussions of the rules and etiquette of golf

www.Legendinc.com
An interesting list of "The 10 Commandments of Golf Etiquette"

www.womensgolf.com
A site devoted to linking women golfers to pertinent sites

www.golfhelp.com
Comprehensive site discussing etiquette and rules

www.golflink.com
State-by-state guide to courses

www.privateclubmemberships.com
A site devoted to buying and selling memberships

golf.about.com
Golf etiquette for beginners

BOOKS

Golf Rules Illustrated
by The USGA

Golf Rules Plain and Simple
by Mark Russell and John Andrisani

The Golfer's Code
by David Gould

Golf Is a Woman's Game
by Jane Horn

The Golf Fitness Handbook
by Gary Wiren

Chapter 5

Equipment

Woods 78
They're made of metal

Irons 80
The long, medium, and short of it

Wedges 82
Depends on the degree of loft

Putters 84
The possibilities are endless

Golf balls 86
Putting a spin on the subject

Golf shoes and gloves 88
Getting a grip on the game

Golf clothes and accessories 90
You might as well look the part

Now what do I do? 92
Answers to common questions

HOW A PRO WOULD PLAY IT

Easy par 4
393 yards

"I'd aim to the left on the fairway and try to set myself up for a 6-iron shot to the green."

woods

The big boys

Take a look into your golf bag. Of the 14 clubs in there, your eye will be drawn to the longest clubs with the biggest heads. These are called **woods**. There are usually three of them, but there can be as many as five. The longest club with the largest head is called **the driver**. Think of it as the 1-wood. The driver is followed by the 2-wood, 3-wood, and all the way up to the 14-wood.

The woods are designed to hit the ball a long way, which is why they are usually used to hit the ball off the tee—though this will depend on the length of the hole and the ability of the golfer. Woods are both the longest in length and lightest of the clubs. These two factors help create the greatest amount of speed in the swing, and that speed will help you power the ball way out onto the fairway. Ultralightweight materials like titanium have allowed the head of the club to get bigger but not heavier. This creates a bigger "sweet spot" much the way a bigger tennis racket creates a bigger area for hitting the ball solidly.

The angle of the face of the driver is called its **loft**. In the typical driver, that angle is practically perpendicular to the ball. That loft is to assure a low, long shot. But it does nothing to ensure accuracy, which is why drives off the tee often go far right or left. For this reason, beginners should opt for a wood with a higher loft. This means the clubface is angled back a little. That little bit of angling means you won't hit the ball as far, but it will be easier to hit more of the ball and thus hit more accurately.

The loft or angle of the clubface has a big impact on the distance you can hit the ball. The driver or 1-wood has the least amount of loft. Each wood after that has a bit more loft.

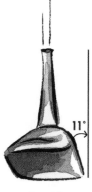

1-wood

11°

1-wood

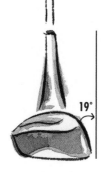

14°

3-wood

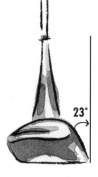

19°

4-wood

23°

5-wood

ASK THE EXPERTS

Why are they still called woods?

Golf is all about tradition. Woods were traditionally made of persimmon wood. These old woods are beautiful—you will still see some in play—but unless they are hit perfectly, they don't offer the same performance as the new metal clubs. Some people call the metal driver simply the driver, and the rest of the "woods" fairway metals, thus avoiding the term wood.

Can you use woods on the fairway?

Sure. That's why there are other woods in your bag. These woods are sometimes called **fairway woods**. The 3-wood has 15 to 16 degrees of loft while the 5-wood has 19 to 21 degrees of loft. The greater the loft, the higher and straighter your ball is supposed to go. That's why many players like to use the 3-wood off the tee.

The driver, also known as the big dog, has the biggest clubhead and the least amount of loft.

FIRST PERSON DISASTER STORY

The wrong clubs at the right time

It was my first big tournament, and I was really psyched. I left the house early and dashed for the club. All excited, I opened the trunk of my car only to realize that those weren't my clubs, but my wife's. I decided I could play with those. Wow, was I wrong. Her clubs were too short for me, and I couldn't swing properly. About the only thing I could do was putt. I played a terrible round and received unmerciful guff from my playing partners. I learned a big lesson: Check your clubs before you play—clean and count them and then put them in the right car.

Jake J., Minneapolis, Minnesota

irons

Elegant tools for the fairway

Golf clubs are like gardening tools in that they all have a specified purpose. If the woods are for distance, then the **irons** are the clubs for accuracy. Their job is to get you from the fairway to as close to the hole as possible. You can have as many as nine irons in a set of golf clubs, starting with the 1-iron, on up to the 9-iron. As the numbers get larger, the club gets shorter, the loft becomes greater, and the ball flies higher. The distance also diminishes, usually about 10 yards between clubs. In other words, if you hit your 6-iron 140 yards, you'll probably hit your 7-iron 130 yards and so on.

It isn't important how far you hit each iron, just that you know how far you hit it. Tiger Woods can hit a 5-iron 220 yards. A senior might hit it 120 yards. And then, of course, we've got everyone in between. The modern iron is **perimeter-weighted**—meaning the weight is around the edges of the face of the iron, not behind it. This allows for a larger sweet spot (where you want the club to strike the ball), making the shot easier to hit.

Most iron sets include the 3- through 9-irons and a pitching wedge.

Materials Matter

While many of the pros on tour prefer steel shafts because they think they are more accurate, the average player is better off with graphite. Yes, they cost more than steel-shafted irons, but graphite shafts are lighter, allowing women and seniors to hit the ball farther. They absorb more of the impact of the shot and feel better to hit. The cost difference between steel and graphite also seems to decrease every year.

An equally important material consideration is whether the iron is forged or cast. A forged iron is made from pounding it into shape. A cast iron is made from a mold. For many golfers, the forged club offers a better feel, but casted irons allow for a greater margin of error.

Iron Deficiency?

In many starter sets, there are only odd-numbered irons: a 3-, 5-, 7-, and 9-iron. You can get by with those for a while. For example, by choking up on the grip or restricting the backswing you can hit a 5-iron 10 yards less to approximate a 6-iron.

Each iron is different from the other by 4 degrees of loft. The idea is that with the same swing, the ball will fly approximately 10 yards more or less, depending on the club you use.

wedges

Salvation is just a chip away

A good many golf shots—some 60 percent in fact—are played within 100 yards of the hole. What's more, nearly half of them are shots from the fairway, the rough, bunkers, and around the edges of the green. These tricky little shots are hit with a **wedge**. The wedge is a club with a very lofted clubface; its job is to get the ball to fly high up in the air and then land so softly on the green that the ball stops dead and doesn't roll off the green. Hit properly, a wedge can get you out of jams and set you up to score.

Almost every set of clubs will contain a **pitching wedge**, a club that can be hit from 100 yards from the green or used right on the edge of the green to chip the ball to the hole. Its loft is around 48 degrees. The second most prevalent wedge is the **sand wedge**, with a loft of about 56 degrees. It is different from the others in that it has a wide flange on the bottom of the club designed to let it glide through the sand, rather than digging in. For average players, the pitching wedge goes 100 yards and the sand wedge 60 yards, leaving a gap in between for a club sometimes called the **gap wedge**, with about 52 degrees of loft. To hit the ball extraordinarily high and soft (so that it stops when it lands on the green), players use a **lob wedge**, with 60 degrees of loft.

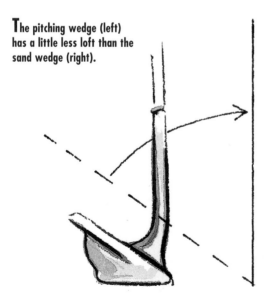
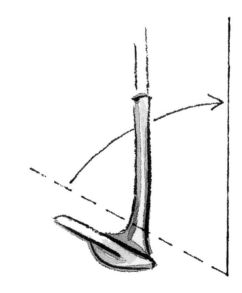

The pitching wedge (left) has a little less loft than the sand wedge (right).

Can the sand wedge be hit from grass as well as sand?

People do it all the time, but remember, the sand wedge is for getting out of trouble, primarily a bunker, also known as a sand trap. It can be used in the rough, even on the fairway, but the flange and high degree of loft make it somewhat more difficult to chip. Need to get the ball up and over a mound or a bunker beside the green? Use the sand wedge. But for normal chipping from off the green, use a pitching wedge.

How many wedges can you carry in your bag?

As many as you want as long as you don't exceed the club limit of 14. Most golfers carry at least two, a pitching and a sand wedge.

The lob wedge looks very strange. How do you hit with it?

This is an intriguing club, but it's a sophisticated weapon better used by a sophisticated player. To hit it 30 yards takes a full swing. It is used to get over trees or out of the deep rough, or to get quickly over a bunker to a small part of the green, but it is difficult to hit correctly because you have to swing so hard.

putters

Your **putter** is the club that you'll use more than any other one. Doubt it? When they talk about a course being par 72—the number of strokes an excellent player would take to play it—about half of those strokes are allocated to putting.

Putting is about feel, confidence, and practice. It doesn't take strength or length or even youth. But confidence and feel are subjective qualities. That may explain why there are so many different styles of putters to choose from. There are long putters, short putters, and some in between. Some golfers have a garage full of putters they've fallen in love with and then divorced.

The two most popular styles of putters are the perimeter-weighted putter and the blade putter. The heavier perimeter-weighted putter has a large "sweet spot," or ideal hitting spot, and thus handles miss-hits better.

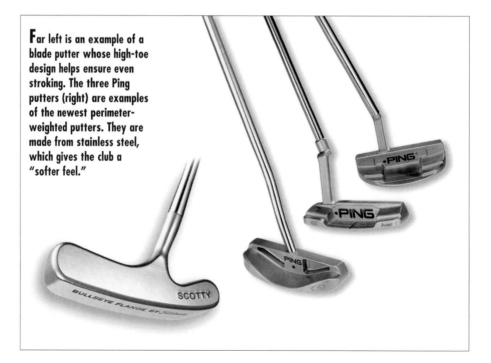

Far left is an example of a blade putter whose high-toe design helps ensure even stroking. The three Ping putters (right) are examples of the newest perimeter-weighted putters. They are made from stainless steel, which gives the club a "softer feel."

Many Shapes, Sizes, and Prices

Because the putter is such a personal tool, manufacturers produce a wide variety of designs. Your main concern is that the putter help you roll the ball into the hole. But it is important that you like the way the putter looks and that it inspires confidence. Good putting is about feel, and you need to feel good about your putter.

The average putter is about 35" long. One odd, but increasingly common, design is the long putter—a putter that is 50" long. There are those who predict that in five years the majority of touring pros will use a long putter. You anchor the end of its handle on either your chin, chest, or belly. This promotes a true pendulum swing, using the shoulders rather than the wrists. (Alas, the wrists are so sensitive it is easy to unconsciously pull them left or right and wreck your shot; shoulders are not nearly so sensitive and keep their alignment.) The long putter takes practice in the beginning, especially on long putts, but some pros suggest if you're starting from scratch, try the long putter.

Putters vary greatly in cost—from $30 to $300. Almost every golf store or pro shop will have a little putting area of plastic grass where you can give various putters a test drive. Beginning golfers will find it easier to choose a putter than a regular club because the basic motion of putting is easier to repeat. They'll know what they like. So don't be shy about trying out different putters until you find the right one for you.

golf balls

Dimpled delights

In the beginning, you shouldn't worry too much about which brand of golf ball you play. In fact, in the beginning you probably won't have the ball long enough to worry about it. You're going to lose golf balls in the woods, in the water, sometimes even in the fairway. You'll need a few dozen to begin with. Figure on taking at least a half dozen to the course with you.

Fortunately, this is not an area that should be hard on your golf budget. Why? You're likely to find as many balls as you lose. There are balls that cost $50 a dozen. You don't need them. Look for balls that cost between $10 and $25 a dozen. Most good golf balls are composed of a cover and an inner core. Ideally, you want a ball with low compression and less spin. For the beginner, spin is the enemy. Ask the salesperson or your pro which balls to buy.

A package of three or four golf balls will be numbered from 1 to 4. Ideally each person in a foursome will use a different-numbered ball. Golf balls also come colored to make finding them a little easier.

ASK THE EXPERTS

What about used balls?

Buy them. The touring pros use a new ball every three holes or so, but then they hit it harder than you. Your ball is likely to last as long as you have it. The general level of performance of all modern golf balls is good. Unless they are obviously scuffed or have been in the water a long time, used balls will perform well and are a prudent investment for the new golfer.

How do I know which ball is mine?

Good question. The best practice is to mark your balls before you head to the course. You can use a Magic Marker pen to put your initial on the ball, or circle the brand name or number. It is your responsibility to be able to identify your ball. So, mark it.

What do I do when I find someone else's ball in the woods?

Common courtesy dictates that you first check to see if someone might be playing the ball—say, in a group coming in the opposite direction on the hole next to yours. If that is the case, then leave it. If you are sure it is no one's ball, then you can pick it up and put it in your bag.

golf shoes and gloves

Giving traction and grip

In a sense, the golf shoe and glove serve the same purpose. They prevent you from slipping. Golf shoes keep your feet in place as you swing. A golf glove keeps the club firmly in your hand when you grip it. The trend in golf shoes is toward casual and comfortable, looking in some cases more like a running or tennis shoe than a classic golf shoe.

While people play golf in athletic shoes, the golf shoe offers more traction. That's because it has cleats and a firmer sole that doesn't twist easily. Golf shoes nowadays are all made with rubber cleats instead of steel spikes. These new cleats are easier on your feet and the golf course and give almost as much grip on the grass as their steel brothers. Most courses now require soft rubber spikes.

Ideally, you want a golf shoe that will also keep your feet dry. There are shoes designed especially for mud and rain, including some golf boots with rubber cleats. Many of the more expensive leather shoes are treated in a way to guarantee they'll keep your feet dry.

You can replace the old spikes on your golf shoes with new ones. A package of new spikes comes with a special tool to get the spikes out.

The Golf Glove

The golf glove looks good, protects your hand from blisters, and helps you grip the club. It's especially helpful in warm weather when your hand is sweating. You wear it on your less dominant hand. If you are right-handed and swing that way, then you wear it on your left hand, and vice versa. The glove is far from necessary. But it seems to give golfers a better grip on the game, both physically and emotionally. (The grip is so much better that baseball players started wearing the golf glove in the 1970s—and eventually modified it into that sport's batting glove.)

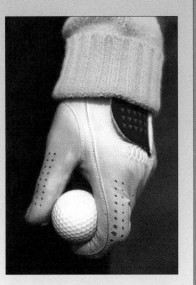

The gloves come in different sizes and materials. Leather gloves are the most expensive, but they offer the best feel of the club. Synthetic gloves are cheaper and last longer. Gloves run between $10 and $20. Beyond the normal golf glove, there are gloves for cold and wet weather. Those are worn on both hands. The gloves to keep your hands warm can look a little like snow mittens. Normally, they slip off to allow you to hit a shot. The wet-weather gloves are cotton and stay on while you're swinging, helping you grip the club securely.

The glove is often the most abused equipment in golf. Many people leave them damp and wadded up in their golf bags when they're finished playing. Don't. Leather gloves crack and deteriorate quickly that way.

golf clothes and accessories

Looking the part

Golf clothing has become a part of casual wear. The golf shirt is so common that it's even become accepted as business wear. Golf clothes can look as though golfers are wearing a uniform, but mainly the clothes make perfect sense, especially items like the vest, which keeps the trunk of your body warm while allowing your limbs freedom to swing.

Since golf is played in all kinds of weather, you need to think in terms of layering clothes, especially in fall, winter, and early spring. Walking and swinging will produce some body heat, so you want to be able to shed layers as necessary. In summer, Bermuda-type shorts and polo or golf shirts are the norm. Khakis for men and women always work. However, tank tops, T-shirts, short-shorts, and jeans are usually off limits.

In cooler times, turtlenecks work well and meet the collared-shirt requirements—the norm at most courses—even though they don't have a collar. For wet weather you'll need some type of rain suit, an umbrella, and a rain hat. Again, layer with a sweater or vest under the suit. Before you hit the course, don't forget your sunscreen, insect repellent, and in colder times, hand cream.

The Golf Bag

A golf bag can hold just about everything you need on the course—but that capacity comes at the cost of extra weight. You should choose your bag carefully. There's a problem if you try to buy a bag shortly after starting to play. You don't yet know whether you'll be a walker or a golf-cart rider. That's the crucial factor in deciding what kind of golf bag you want.

The bigger, more spacious golf bags work better when you don't have to carry them—or even drag them along with a pull cart. A bag designed for a cart might weigh eight pounds. One you carry should weigh half that. The bigger bag has more pockets in which to put everything, from a sweater to a sandwich to sunscreen. (Drinks are usually kept in the golf cart; most have soft-drink holders built into them.)

Lighter bags tend to have fewer pockets for storing tees, gloves, tissues, you name it. They're also made out of lighter materials that can tear more easily than those on heavier bags—a consideration for longevity. A lighter bag will usually have a stand, however, that automatically kicks out to hold it up when you put the bag on the ground. This keeps it out of the mud and grass and means you don't have to bend over to pick it up. The light bags often have double straps so you carry them like backpacks. Big or small, bags range in price from $60 to $160 and up. The bag you choose all depends on your needs and budget.

Some bags have legs that automatically pop out when the bottom of the bag touches the ground. This keeps the bag off wet grass and makes picking clubs a whole lot easier.

now what do I do?

I'm nervous about buying my first set of clubs. What if I get the wrong one?

Don't be afraid to shop around and ask for advice. Many big golf stores offer netted stalls where you can actually hit balls with the various clubs. Some may even have experts who can help you get the right clubs—ones that have the right length, shaft flex, and grip size for you. Look at starter sets. They'll give you an idea of the basics. Help can be as close as your local golf course where the professional staff can advise you about clubs. Or you can try your local sports store or a large sports outlet. Once you know your length of club, you can even buy clubs online. For used clubs, consider **www.ebay.com**.

Do I need one of those big titanium drivers?

Not when you're getting started. The 3-wood is a better club off the tee. The big drivers hit the ball farther, but farther can also mean farther off line and off the fairway. The big drivers are also expensive, ranging from $100 to $500. Better to wait and see how committed you are to the game, and just what kind of driver in terms of its loft and length you can handle. The longer the shaft and lower the loft, the farther the ball will go, but the more difficult the shot will be to hit.

I noticed that some women pro players use woods on all their fairway shots. Why?

Many of the women on the LPGA tour play with four or more woods in their golf bag. Thanks to the loft on fairway woods, the ball gets easily up in the air without your having to "lift" it there as you would if you used an iron. Strong players can get the ball in the air with a long iron. Some women and seniors struggle with this. So do beginners.

Which specialty clubs should I add to my starter set?

Think about adding a lofted metal wood, like a 7- or 9-wood. These can help get you out of trouble and they're easier to hit than long irons. There are also clubs called rescue clubs that are designed for long grass and tough lies. Some are a hybrid between a wood and an iron and look a little like each. Beyond that, you could look at wedges, maybe a lob wedge for extremely high shots. Some golfers even carry two putters, one with a long handle for short putts and one with a short handle for long putts. The variety of clubs is tremendous, but remember, the limit is 14 to a bag.

I'm left-handed. Are there golf clubs out there for me?

Yes, there are! Just ask your pro or sports store owner about them.

Helpful Resources

WEB SITES

www.golfreview.com
A chance to see what others think of clubs

www.golfshoppingguide.com
An electronic golf mall

golf.about.com/library/weekly/aa112402a.htm
A look at how your skill level determines what clubs you carry

BOOKS

Total Golf
by Mike Adams and T.J. Tomasi, the Academy of Golf at PGA National

The Women's Guide to Golf
by Kellie Stenzel Garvin

How Golf Clubs Really Work and How to Optimize Their Designs
by Frank D. Werner

Chapter 6

Teeing Off

Using the driver 96
Hitting the ball on the upswing

The grip 98
Where it all begins

The stance 100
Get in an athletic position

The backswing 102
Make it all of one piece

The downswing 104
How to do it right

The follow through 106
It tells the story

Common tee-off errors 108
Any way you slice it

Now what do I do? 110
Answers to common questions

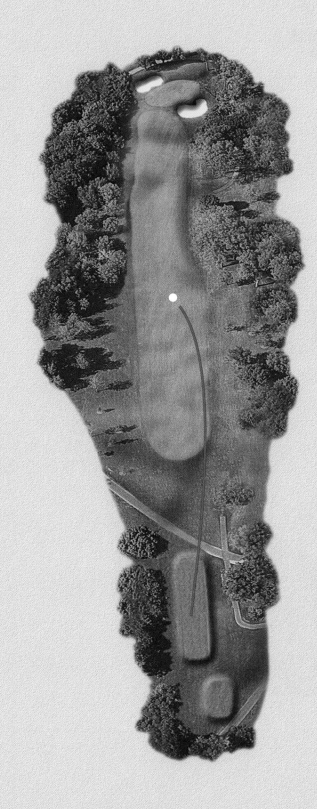

HOW A PRO
WOULD PLAY IT

**Medium par 4
420 yards**

"I'd hit toward the right—the slope of the fairway will help the ball roll toward the middle."

using the driver

Big and dangerous

On the tee, you're given the advantage of hitting your shot off a three-inch-long wooden peg also known, somewhat confusingly, as a tee. Take it. The tee shot is the big kahuna of golf. Although this is always the longest shot on a hole, you won't necessarily be hitting a driver (the 1-wood with the largest head). On a short par 3, for instance, you'll likely be hitting an iron.

In fact, some pros think you should avoid the driver in the beginning. On longer holes you'll have more success using a 3-wood or a 5-wood than a big-headed driver, which is difficult to hit straight. Why is the driver so hard to hit well? Because it has very little angle (or loft) on its clubface. That means it's very unforgiving if you don't hit the ball directly in the middle of the clubface. Few hit the ball square, and the result is a bit of a spin, sending the ball left or right. Why is this a big deal? A ball hit 10 yards too far to the left with a 3-wood would be off by 20 yards if you had used the driver.

Working with a pro can help you start out using the driver correctly.

ASK THE EXPERTS

Where should I tee-up my ball?

You must tee-up your ball between the tee markers. Most golfers choose a spot in the middle of the markers. But check out the hole in front of you. If trouble (a water hazard or a clump of trees) is on the right, place your tee closer to the right tee marker while aiming your shot to the left. Do the opposite if the trouble is on the left. Note: You cannot tee the ball ahead of the markers, but you can go up to two club-lengths behind them if you want.

How high do I tee it?

Get the ball high enough that its top half sits above the top edge of your driver when the clubhead is on the ground behind the ball. If you want to hit the ball lower, then tee it lower, and so on. Even when you have a short hole and can use a short iron, take advantage of the wooden tee. Just remember to tee it lower when using an iron. An iron shot will usually chop a tee in half. That's why many golfers use broken tees for their iron shots on par 3s—as they already want to tee it lower than normal.

What is the fascination with the driver?

The driver is the lightest and longest club in your bag, and it has the least amount of loft on its face, all of which makes the ball go farther if you hit it square. It's fun to hit the ball far, but while far is fun, don't overlook the value of hitting the ball straight. Otherwise, you'll be looking for your ball in the weeds and tall trees.

the grip

Firm without crushing

Most pros consider your grip the foundation of your game. A poor grip may lead to a poor swing. That's why you need to master the grip before you can graduate to the swing. There are three basic grips; no one is considered "correct." It's up to you to find the one that works best for you. The three basic grips are the **Vardon**, the **interlocking,** and the **doublehanded grip**, sometimes called the baseball grip.

The Vardon grip is the one recommended for beginners with average-size hands. The latter two are best for small hands. What's the difference between the three grips? With the Vardon your right pinky finger overlaps your left index finger as you fit your hands snugly around the club shaft. The interlocking grip uses the same position, but you interlock your right pinky with your left forefinger. The doublehanded grip is akin to a baseball-bat grip—in other words, the hands and fingers don't overlap.

The grip is both simple and critical. You will use basically the same grip for all of your shots. Remember, you aren't choking the club, you're holding it. Legendary pro Sam Snead always said you should grip the club as if it were a small bird—with enough pressure to keep it from flying away but without too much pressure to hurt it.

Because the grip is so critical to your game, you owe it to yourself to have a pro show you exactly how it works.

This teaching club has a preformed grip to help you place your fingers properly around the club.

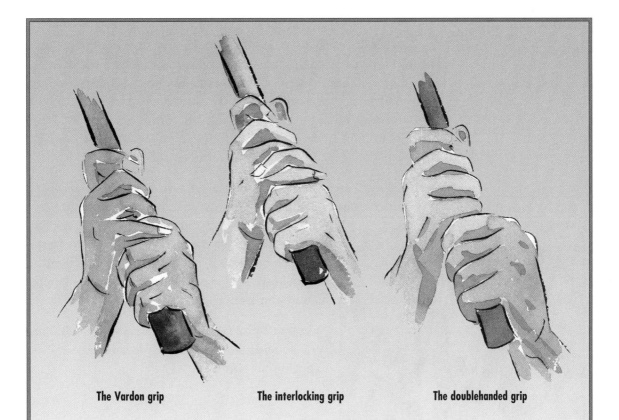

The Vardon grip   The interlocking grip   The doublehanded grip

Hands On: The Vardon Grip

Assuming you are right-handed, place your left hand on the club as if you were shaking hands with it. Hold the club in front of you. Turn the club's face so it points in the direction you want to hit the ball. The thumb of your left hand should run down the center of the shaft, and you should be able to see only the first two knuckles on your left hand. If you are doing this right, you are not gripping the club with the palm of your hand but with the ends of your fingers.

Now place your right hand on the club. Remember, the hands work together. The club is a little more in the fingers of the right hand than the left. The right thumb slides over the left thumb so that the lifeline of your right palm fits over your left thumb. Next the little finger of your right hand fits between the forefinger and index finger of your left hand.

The crease, or V, created between your left thumb and index finger should point between your chin and right ear. Similarly, the crease, or V, between your right thumb and index finger should point between your right shoulder and right ear. Practice is vital. Leave a club in your bedroom or your office, and practice the grip until it gets natural.

the stance

Addressing the ball

You know where you want to hit the ball. But how do you get it there? For starters, you need to line up your shot. A lot of golfers hit the ball off course because they don't line up their body to the target. To line up correctly, you must place your feet, hips, and shoulders parallel to the target you want the ball to reach. To see if you're aligned correctly, take a club and, with two hands, hold it out in front of you parallel to the target line. It will show you if your shoulders, for example, are lined up right.

Once you are lined up, you need to get your body into the proper **athletic stance** before you swing. In golf, the stance is about balance. Your knees are flexed slightly, and your body weight is evenly distributed between the balls of your left and right foot. (A lot of beginners put their weight on their toes or heels; try to keep your weight centered on the balls of your feet.)

Now gently place the clubhead behind the ball. This is called **addressing the ball**. It means you are about to begin your swing.

The classic stance of addressing the ball.

ASK THE EXPERTS

How do I establish the target line?

You stand behind the ball and look at the target, visualizing where on the hole you want the ball to go. Then it is a matter of setting up parallel to that line. On the practice range it is helpful to lay a club down near your toes and see if you are lined up properly. A club across your chest will do the same thing. Don't just assume you are aligned properly. There is a good chance you aren't.

Where should the ball be in relation to my stance?

This is called **ball position**, and it varies when you use different clubs. When you use the driver, the ball should be lined up with the heel of your left foot. Ball position for irons is in the middle, except for the 2- and 3-irons—they should be one inch forward of center.

What is a closed stance?

Depending on the shot, you will need to adjust your stance. A straight hole calls for a normal drive with a square stance, meaning your feet line up parallel to your target. If you need to curve your drive (say, to avoid a water hazard or a clump of trees), then you need to change your stance. A closed stance simply means your body is aimed to the right of your intended target. That does not necessarily mean the ball will go there.

the backswing

The art of the arc

Okay, you're lined up and good to go. Now what? Get ready to swing. How exactly do you do this properly? The swing is divided into several parts. The first part is called the **backswing** (this is where you pull your club back from the ball); the second part is the **downswing** (where you swing down to hit it); and the last part is the **follow through** (the completion of your swing after you've hit the ball). Ideally, if you get it right, your swing should be one fluid motion and your club an extension of your arms and hands.

When you begin the backswing, pros advise that your shoulders, arms, and hands all move as one unit. This is called a **one-piece takeaway**. This fluid movement hopefully assures that rather than succumbing to the temptation to pick the club off the ground, you let your whole upper body gently drag the club off the ground. Your goal now is to keep bringing the club back smoothly, as if it were doing this of its own accord.

Beginning golfers are so keen on hitting the ball that they move too quickly through the takeaway and backswing. Take your time and gently drag your club off the ground. Do it in super slow motion, until you feel the movement.

Keep your left arm extended as you swing back and shift your weight to your right leg.

Your shoulders should be turned 90 degrees.

FIRST PERSON DISASTER STORY

A bad case of the yips

I decided to study up on my swing during the winter months when the weather ruled out any golf. I avidly read the golf magazines and never missed the shows on the Golf Channel. My wife gave me a couple of great golf instructional books for Christmas. By the time I hit the course in the spring, I had so many new and different swings to think about I got a case of the yips—I was so afraid to make the "wrong" swing, I couldn't even hit the ball. I'd get to the top of the swing and I literally couldn't move. Talk about paralysis by analysis. I went right over to my golf pro, who helped me focus on my swing and put aside all the many shoulds and coulds I had read about but not tried. Learning is great, but don't take in too much information. Try each tip one at a time. And listen to only one voice.

Lucas M., Santa Fe, New Mexico

the downswing

No, it's not jazz

When you set up for your stance, your weight was evenly divided between your feet. Now, as your bring your club back farther, your weight should shift, and more should be placed on your right foot and less on your left. In fact, at the very top of your backswing, 80 to 90 percent of your weight should be on your right foot and 10 to 20 percent on the left. Some golfers let the heel of their left foot come off the ground.

The goal is to have most of your weight behind the golf ball so that when you swing down you will hit it with maximum power. Because most of your weight is on the right side, your right leg must hold firm—no bending it out.

Another key point to bear in mind is your shoulders. Your shoulders need to turn a full 90 degrees. Your hands should be cocked or hinged almost at a 90-degree angle. The better the hinge, the more power you will have when you hit the ball.

When you reach the pinnacle of your backswing, it's time to bring the club down and release all the power you have stored up in your right leg and right arm. During this downswing, your body mirrors the movements it made on the backswing: Your weight should shift from your right foot to your left, and only the toe of your right foot is on the ground.

On impact with the ball, your weight should shift to your left foot.

ASK THE EXPERTS

I can't seem to get the hang of the backswing. It feels so strange. What am I doing wrong?

Maybe nothing. The golf swing is not the most natural of swings. It takes a lot of practice to "feel right." But because the swing feels awkward at first, it is easy to introduce errors into your swing and not know it. That's why it's important to work on your swing with a pro who can check that you are doing everything correctly. The swing is something that is very hard to self-diagnose. You need another pair of eyes to tell you what errors you are committing.

My pro says I am doing everything right, but my ball doesn't seem to go very far. How can I gain distance?

Increase the speed of your downswing. The faster you can swing the club down, the farther your shot will go. And keep your wrists cocked until the last moment when you hit the ball. Make sure your downswing continues past the point of hitting the ball so that your right arm finishes high up over your left shoulder. You also might want to consider whether you are hitting the ball squarely or not. A short swing that squarely hits the ball will produce more distance than a long, loopy swing that doesn't make solid contact.

the follow through

The big finish

The **follow through** is everything that happens after you have hit the ball. How your body ends up can tell you a lot about how you hit the ball. If you can make a swing where you end up balanced and facing the target, then you have finished in good shape. Is your belt buckle facing the target? Have your knees come together? Is your right shoulder a little lower? That is a perfect finish. Pros suggest you hold this pose until the ball has landed.

Instead of maintaining their posture throughout the swing, most beginners straighten up when they hit the ball. A good follow through has your head, chest, and hips facing the target and most of your weight (about 90 percent) on your left foot, your right foot acting almost like a rudder to help keep your balance. A good follow through has been compared with a gymnast "sticking" the end of a difficult routine. If you can get to a good balanced finish, there is a chance that you made a good swing. So work on a good finish, and your swing will improve as well.

ASK THE EXPERTS

What is the single most common error golfers make regarding the swing?

Trying to hit the ball too hard. When you do that, you force your swing. Your goal is to find a tempo; practice and it will come.

How far should the club go in the follow through? I've seen people who practically have the club wrapped up around their necks when they are done.

A number of pros suggest that you work on making your follow through bigger and longer. If you are trying for a bigger follow through, it will automatically create a bigger backswing.

A good finish calls for good footwork. At the end of your swing, your right foot should be up on its toes.

common tee-off errors

There are quite a few common errors that every single beginner makes. Don't fret, just relax and know that errors are all part of the fun of learning the game.

Not hitting the ball squarely Connecting directly with the ball is not easy. Often golfers contact only the top of the ball, or miss the ball altogether. (This is known as a whiff.) Sometimes the ball connects with the heel of the club, sometimes the toe; either way the ball will miss the target.

Solution: Keep your eye on the ball and concentrate. Try sticking a tee in the ground and practice hitting just the tee. Then add the ball. Also, go easy. Don't try to hit the ball too hard.

Slicing or hooking the ball The ball curves either too far right or too far left due to improper clubhead rotation.

Solution: Check your wrist position. Chances are your grip is too tight. Relax!

Swinging inside out or outside in Your club path should be a bit like a pendulum: straight back, straight down. When your club path isn't "straight," but curves from the inside out or outside in, your ball will go off course.

Solution: Most golfers have a bit of one or the other. Work on balance: Visualize a swinging pendulum when you swing.

Pushing and pulling You push the ball too far right or pull it too far left because your body is either too far in front of your club or too far behind it.

Solution: Check your ball position and your body position.

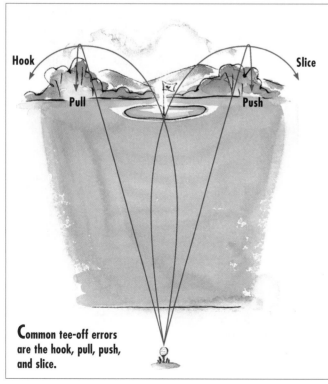

Hook Slice

Pull Push

Common tee-off errors are the hook, pull, push, and slice.

ASK THE EXPERTS

When should I see a pro for help?

If you are consistently slicing or hooking the ball during a round of golf, see a pro before you play again. You don't want bad techniques to become bad habits. Find out what you are doing wrong before your body gets used to it and thinks it's "natural."

I can't seem to get a handle on the proper grip. How do I fix this?

It's perfectly normal for a new golf grip to feel uncomfortable at first. Just keep practicing. You can also ask your pro about a "teaching club" that helps new golfers get a better handle on their grip and swing. It's a specially weighted club that has a fitted grip. You can't put your hands in the wrong place, and the weight in the clubhead helps you feel your swing.

I keep making the same mistake! No matter how hard I try, I can't seem to fix it! What should I do?

Chances are you're trying too hard. The biggest mistake beginners make is getting mentally uptight over the swing and consequently getting physically uptight to boot. Relax. Breathe. Hum when you swing; try to feel the rhythm of it. Forget all the dos and don'ts, and just be in the moment of the swing.

I really want my drives to go far. The harder I hit them, the less distance they travel. What is going on?

One of the big errors beginners make is to assume that they are the power behind their shots. That's why you feel you have to hit the ball hard or hit it so you lift it up in the air. Right? Wrong. Your club is the real power. Use it. Let your club do the work, and get out of the way.

now what do I do?

Why is mastering the swing so hard?

Part of the appeal of golf is its difficulty. If you're ever to the point that you think you have the swing mastered, then cherish that moment, for surely it won't last long. The swing has been the life study of many great players. Once you have gotten the physical fundamentals down (grip, stance, and swing), consider tapping into your mental powers. Try to mentally visualize your swing before you make it. Next visualize your ball landing on target.

Why do my friends keep saying, "Keep your head still and your left arm straight"?

These ancient words of advice are good ideas, but over the years they have become a bit overstated and simplified. Your head can move slightly as you take your backswing, and it can turn toward the target on the follow through. At the moment of impact, however, it needs to be positioned behind the ball. Look at pictures of the great players. They have that position in common. As far as the left arm, it needs to be extended but not necessarily straight. It can't be tense.

How far back do I swing the club?

You want to turn your shoulders and extend your left arm. Your left shoulder can come to rest under your chin. But don't take the club back too far. Most pros think that when it reaches parallel to the ground, that's plenty.

What if I'm not brushing the grass on my practice swings?

You probably are not maintaining the posture you had when you addressed the ball. If you maintain your posture, you can even close your eyes and get a consistent brush on the grass with the club. Do this and you'll get good contact.

Does my tall height affect my swing?

Everything affects your swing. If you are unusually tall or short, study the swings of professional golfers who match your build and height. Also, make sure your clubs are properly matched to your body size (see pages 12–13). If your clubs are too short, you will need to stand too close to the ball for a proper swing. Likewise, if they are too long, you will need to stand too far away from the ball.

Helpful Resources

WEB SITES

PGAProfessional.com
A Web site with a special section devoted to golf tips and lessons

Golf101.com
Lots of help here, too

BOOKS

Golf Skills
by Roger Hyder

How to Find Your Perfect Golf Swing
by Rick Smith

The PGA Manual of Golf
by Rick Martino

Teach Yourself Golf
by Bernard Gallacher and Mark Wilson

Tiger Woods: How I Play Golf
by Tiger Woods

The Golf Handbook
by Vivien Saunders

The Greatest Game Ever Played: Harry Vardon, Francis Ouimet, and the Birth of Modern Golf
by Mark Frost

Harvey Penick's Little Red Book: Lessons and Teachings from a Lifetime in Golf
by Harvey Penick

Power Golf for Women: How to Hit Longer and Straighter from Tee to Green
by Jane Horn

Chapter 7

The Fairway Shot

Using the irons 114
And what about fairway woods?

The short irons 116
They actually are shorter

The stance 118
Developing a nice balance

The swing 120
Getting the ball up by hitting down

Difficult lies 122
Rough, uneven lies, etc.

Now what do I do? 124
Answers to common questions

HOW A PRO
WOULD PLAY IT

Difficult par 4
391 yards

"I'd avoid looking at the water, keep my head down and hit a low drive under the wind."

using the irons

Precision instruments

Irons are more precise than their larger brothers, the woods. For one thing, there are more of them—the higher the iron number, the shorter the distance it hits the ball. Irons number from 1 through 9, each club a half-inch longer than the next, and each clubface more open than the next. The iron with the steepest clubface is the 1-iron; the iron with the most open clubface (or loft) is the 9-iron. Those irons that range from 1 to 4 are called the **long irons**. A 1-iron will go lower and farther, a 9-iron higher and shorter. The 1-iron, however, is very difficult to hit accurately. Most golf sets start with the 3-iron and go on up to the 9-iron.

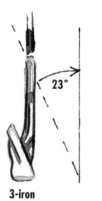
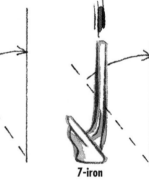

3-iron   4-iron   5-iron   6-iron   7-iron

The loft or angle of the clubface determines the distance and accuracy of your shot. The 3-iron has less loft (23 degrees) than the pitching wedge (about 55 degrees).

On the fairway, you won't be able to use a wooden tee. Still, you'll need to get the ball in the air, especially the closer you get to the hole. The irons are designed to get the ball in the air, especially the **mid-irons** (5 through 7) and the **short irons** (8 and 9). Let the loft and length of the club do the work for you. A common mistake beginners make is trying to "scoop" or lift the ball in the air. There is no need to do that. The club is designed to lift the ball for you. So let it do its job.

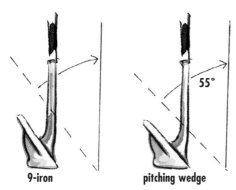

9-iron   **pitching wedge**

55°

What About Fairway Woods?

There is an old golf joke that in an electrical storm, you should grab your 1-iron and hold it high in the air. As the punch line goes: "for not even God can hit a 1-iron."

It takes strength and clubhead speed to get the ball in the air with the long irons. You're better off with a fairway wood. (They range in number as high as 14.) They can hit the ball as far as long irons (a 7-wood substituting for a 4-iron, for example) but in addition go higher and softer, which is important when you're trying to get a ball to land on a green. They also can be much easier for the average player to hit. They have more loft and a bigger sweet spot than the long irons. Traditionally, golfers carried a 3-wood as well as the driver. Then the 5-wood started to replace the 2- and 3-irons. Now many golfers—especially beginners—don't use any iron longer than a 5.

the short irons

How to come up short

Your scores will drop dramatically when you can consistently hit the ball on the green from 120 yards in. The 8- and 9-irons can be your best friends. On a particularly long and difficult hole they allow you to lay up short of danger to a distance you like—say, 100 yards—and from there you can most likely hit it onto the green. Know your distances. Practice your short irons at the range with a three-quarter swing—that means taking the clubhead back to about 10 o'clock instead of the full 12 o'clock. You need a narrow stance, good balance, and a steady swing.

Short irons are used when near the green.

Playing into the Wind

Sometimes, when the wind is really howling, you'll need to keep the ball low even if you're 100 yards from the green and would normally hit a high pitching wedge (see page 130). Pull out your 9-iron. You need to hit what is called a knock-down shot, a low shot that doesn't roll very far. You place the ball farther back in your stance toward the right foot. You move your hands ahead of the ball, delofting the club. You avoid swinging too hard because that will just make the ball go up in the air. Shorter backswing, shorter follow through, easy does it. This is a shot you'll need to try at the range before you're called upon to make it on the course.

Playing in the Rain

Here's the good news: You can continue to play so long as there isn't any lightning and the greenskeeper hasn't come around in his or her cart to tell you that the course is now closed. So how do you play in the rain? First of all, get out your golf umbrella. It should be large enough to cover you and your clubs (that is why they are so huge). Next get out your golf bag cover (which comes with the bag). Put it over your clubs to keep the grips dry. Hopefully, you'll have a small towel in your bag that you can use to dry your face and hands so your grip doesn't slip.

the stance

A balanced approach

With the long and mid-irons, your feet are going to be a little closer together when addressing the ball than when you are teeing up with a driver (see page 96). You'll position yourself so the ball is farther back than the middle of your stance. The higher the number on the iron you are using, the farther back in your stance the ball will be. For the longer irons and fairway woods, the ball should be opposite the spot of the logo on most sport shirts.

Unlike the driver, where you have a little more weight on the right side at address, the weight for irons is more equally distributed over each foot. Because each iron is a half-inch shorter than the one before, you'll have to stand a little closer to the ball as the number on the iron gets higher. Don't forget to flex your knees slightly. Standing tall, drop your hands down toward your knees. They should be more than a fist, but less than two fists, away from your body. Your shoulders should be level.

Golf pros talk a lot about ball positioning. This is the fine art of placing your feet in the proper position behind the ball.

Ball position for:

Short iron
Long iron
Tee shot

Do I change my grip for the irons and fairway woods?

For all shots, except the putt, the grip remains pretty much the same. Check the V formed by the connection between your thumb and index finger. On the left hand it should point somewhere between your chin and right ear. On the right hand, between your right ear and right shoulder. From address, you should also be able to see at least two knuckles on your left hand.

What if I don't move the ball back in my stance?

Remember positioning the ball off your left heel for the driver? You need to get it back more toward the center of your swing for the mid- and short irons. Having the ball farther back will promote a descending blow and allow the ball to get up in the air with spin. That in turn keeps your ball from rolling off when it hits the green.

What's this about weight transfer?

Throw a baseball. You'll transfer your weight to your right side and then to your left. A pitcher using just his arm wouldn't be able to throw very hard. The same idea applies to golf. Use your whole body when you transfer your weight from right to left. Let it happen naturally.

the swing

Making irons sing

Golf is a game of opposites. Swing left and the ball goes to the right. Swing down and the ball goes up. With the woods you want power, with the irons accuracy. Irons also get the ball reasonably high in the air, allowing it to land softly on the green so it stops and doesn't roll off the green. This is the main reason you hit an iron from the fairway. You don't want to "lift" the ball in the air. Let the club do the work for you.

"**H**inged" wrists are key when using the irons.

For the iron to work properly, you need to have a strong descending downswing that bites into the ball. Your grip is key. Your wrists must be correctly "hinged," or bent at the upswing, so you can snap your wrists when you bring the club down. The proof that you've hit the shot with a descending blow is in the **divot**—the patch of grass that comes popping out from in front of the ball as you send it soaring. The high loft of the clubface will make the ball go high, and the downward blow will give it backspin, which helps it set down softly on the green and brings it to a quick halt.

ASK THE EXPERTS

How do I know how far away I am from the green?

Most courses have stakes or other types of markers on each side of the fairway marking the distance at 100, 150, and 200 yards. Sometimes the marker is embedded in the ground. Distance could also be marked on the heads of sprinklers. You can use a large stride to measure a yard and find the distance between your ball and the marker. All yardage markers, unless otherwise noted, measure to the center of the green.

I am pretty close to the green. What should I do?

Consider trying a three-quarter swing with a short iron. With the three-quarter shot, you don't take the club all the way back as you do for a full swing. You stop the swing three-quarters of the way up and only slightly shift your weight from the right leg and then back to the left. Think of this as a baby swing. Why do it? Because when the ball hits the green it will stay there and not continue to roll past the pin.

FIRST PERSON DISASTER STORY

Don't lose your club or your cool

I received a very special wristwatch for a very special occasion, my 20th wedding anniversary. I wore it to the course by mistake, but took it off at the first tee and carefully put it into my golf bag. All was well until the 6th hole when I hit a ball in the water and in disgust threw my iron against the side of the bag. I wasn't proud of myself, but I'd done that before. No big deal. Until, of course, I went to retrieve my watch at the end of the game. Somehow the watch-face had gotten shattered. I thought back to my fit of rage. Anger on the course can be costly in so many ways.

Kip L., Hayward, California

difficult lies

The ups and downs of a golf course

You're used to hitting the ball off a consistent and usually artificial grass surface at the range. Life isn't like that out on the course. The reality is you'll find all kinds of unsettling spots on the golf course. They are what golfers call **difficult lies**, meaning your ball is not sitting nicely on a tuft of grass but is on a hill or stuck in some weeds or, worse yet, on top of a divot that someone forgot to replace. Don't panic. First, inspect the lie to see what you're up against. If you've landed on a really bare surface—often called a tight lie—you'll need to hit the ball cleanly. How? Choose an iron with a lofted head, say, an 8- or 9-iron, and keep your weight more on your left side. You may also try choking down on the grip a bit.

In tall grass, long irons are a no-no because the tall grass grabs the club and twists it. Grab a high-lofted 8- or 9-iron to get out of the mess. Your priority should be getting back in the short grass, not hitting a long shot.

Uneven lies, such as the one shown here, make for a more challenging course.

Downhill, Uphill, and Side-hill Lies

A golf course isn't flat. You'll find the ball resting on the slope of a steep hill, while the driving range is strictly flat lies. The secret is to try to make the lie flat by changing your posture.

The uphill lie: Get your knees, hips, and shoulders parallel to the ground. Keep the ball in the middle of your stance, and allow your swing to follow the contour of the ground. Try to keep your balance.

The downhill lie: Get your knees, hips, and shoulders parallel with the downhill slope. Put the ball back in your stance. You'll need to use a higher-lofted club to get the ball in the air. You'll also want to grip down on the club a little, getting closer to the clubface, or choking up, as you would in baseball. Take a few extra practice swings to simulate what you'll need to do. As you swing, follow the contour of the ground; don't try to lift the ball out.

The side-hill lie: In this case, the ball can be on a hill either above your feet or below your feet. The ball will tend to fly left above your feet and right below them. Compensate with your aim. Get good balance. When the ball is above your feet, grip down on the club and put the ball back in your stance. When the ball is below your feet, stand closer to the ball and put it forward in your stance. Think about using a shorter iron than the distance might suggest. Use a three-quarter swing.

now what do I do?

What if I don't take a divot with my irons?

As long as you are brushing the grass and hitting the ball squarely, you don't have to take a divot. The more you hit the ball with a descending blow, the more likely you are to take a divot and get spin on the ball. If you're taking divots, inspect them. Their direction can tell you about the path of your swing. They shouldn't be too big or deep; they should be about the width of a strip of bacon on up to a dollar bill.

How do I keep the ball low if there is a lot of wind?

Many of the great players have come from Texas: Ben Hogan, Byron Nelson, Justin Leonard. They battled the wind and became better golfers for it. To avoid being blown off by the wind, strive to hit a low shot with little loft. Position the ball farther back toward your right foot. Take a lower-lofted club, say a 5-iron, and swing it easier than usual, or take a three-quarter swing.

My 8-iron goes the same distance as my 5-iron. Why is that?

According to the laws of physics, they can't go the same distance with the same swing. The problem is you aren't making good contact with either club. It could be you are over-swinging. Work on hitting the ball solidly before you worry how far the ball is going with each club. Once you've made solid contact, the variance in distances will be obvious.

I like to play year-round. How do I deal with the rain?

You're lucky if you can play all year. Rain shouldn't stop you. You need good rain gear, a bucket-style hat, and some kind of hood to go over your clubs. Your main concern will be gripping the clubs. There are cotton gloves that work very well in rain; the wetter they get, the better you grip the club. You wear them on both hands. They're really essential.

My set of irons came with a 3-iron. Should I use a fairway wood instead?

Try the long irons, but you may prefer a 7-wood or one of the other utility woods. One of the top professional players, Vijay Singh, carries a 7-wood on tour. It has more loft, a bigger head, and more weight near the sole. It all adds up to an easier club to hit, and it is designed to get the ball up in the air quickly.

Helpful Resources

WEB SITES

Sportsillustrated.com/golfonline/instruction
Variety of good golf tips

BOOKS

101 Essential Tips in Golf
by Peter Ballingall

Dave Pelz's Short Game Bible: Master the Finesse Swing and Lower Your Score
by Dave Pelz, with James A. Frank
The first in a series of books on the short game, by a former NASA research analyst

Chapter 8

The Approach Shot

The chip shot 128
How to get to the green

The pitch shot 130
Send the ball soaring

Using the sand wedge 132
Getting out of a bunker

Now what do I do? 134
Answers to common questions

HOW A PRO
WOULD PLAY IT

Very difficult par 4
404 yards

"I'd hit a 3-wood or long iron off the tee and then use a short iron to the green."

the chip shot

The most important shot in golf

You've taken your shot from the fairway with a goal of hitting it on the green. Although a worthy goal, you may have found yourself missing the green. That's okay. Most players do. Even the best players on the professional tour only average landing on about 13 of 18 greens **in regulation** (the prescribed number of shots according to par) on each round. And yet they are consistently under par, meaning they are getting the ball on the green with their chip shot and close enough to the hole that they can make their putt. This is called "getting up and down," probably the single most important facet of scoring.

So you didn't quite get the ball onto the green. Now you're left with a shot that is about 10 yards from the hole. What do you do? You make a chip shot—a nifty little shot that, if done right, has your ball spending less time in the air and more time rolling on the green, hopefully toward the cup.

What club do you use to perform this amazing feat of precision and poise? Any of your short irons will do the job. Here's a general guide. Using an 8-iron will produce a shot where the ball flies about 25 percent of the distance and rolls 75 percent; a pitching wedge is about 40 percent air, 60 percent roll; and a sand wedge is about 50 percent air, 50 percent roll.

Ball position is important in the chip shot. You want the ball back by your right foot. Use a putting grip.

The backswing on the chip shot is short, only about knee high—the same for the follow through. Also, try not to release your wrists or scoop the ball up in the air. You want it to roll in a chip shot.

How Do I Chip?

In hitting this shot, you want the ball positioned back toward your right foot. As you swing, 60 percent of your weight is on your left foot, and there is no weight shift during the swing. Don't try to lift the ball. Keep your left wrist firm through impact; don't let it bend or break down, a true indication that you're trying to scoop the ball. You can grip the club like you do the other clubs, or grip it like your putter (see page 142). Keep your hands relaxed. Visualize the shot: where it will hit on the green and how it will roll to the hole. Make a practice swing to see and feel just that. You should finish your chip shot with the head of the club low to the ground.

A common error that beginners often make is to not follow through enough. They stop their follow through where the ball used to be. Be sure to finish your swing. Apply the swing rule: You should have the same distance on your follow through as you did on your backswing. If you take the club back two feet, you should finish two feet past the ball as well.

the pitch shot

Getting the ball high and on the green

Here is a pretty good general rule for around the green: Putt when you can putt, chip when you can't putt, and pitch when you can't chip. The modern golf course has many humps and bumps around the greens, not to mention areas filled with sand and water. Yikes! If the distance between your ball and the edge of the green is more than a third of the way between you and the flagstick, you'll need to consider the pitch shot. To make this shot, you will need a high-lofted club such as the pitching wedge, sand wedge, or even a club known as the lob wedge. Unlike with the chip shot, the goal here is to have your ball spend more time in the air and less time rolling on the ground.

In the pitch shot, the ball is positioned in the middle of the stance, and the club is taken back about 45 degrees.

Whereas the chip shot allows you very little body movement, the pitch shot calls for a half swing. Keep your weight and hands centered. The wider your stance, the farther the ball will go. For a higher trajectory have your ball positioned more toward the left foot. Cock your wrists on the backswing. The important thing is that the club never slow down. Try to envision the club sliding under the ball. Keep everything moving, matching your follow through to your backswing.

using the sand wedge

Hitting the sand, not the ball

Sand on a golf course is meant to be a hazard. Sure, you will try to avoid sand traps, but everyone lands in them, even the pros. Once in a bunker or a sand trap, don't panic. The sand shot isn't as difficult as it looks. First of all, you've got a club specifically designed for the job: the **sand wedge**. The beefy flat flange on the bottom of the club is shaped to allow the club to glide through the sand, not dig down into it as other clubs would do. (In fact, you are not allowed to touch the sand with your club prior to swinging at the ball.)

How do you use this club? First you want to have both an open stance and an open clubface. The open stance means your shoulders and feet are aimed slightly to the left of your target. The open clubface means your sand wedge is aimed slightly to the right. Take a half swing, and follow through an equal distance.

The open clubface of your sand wedge will allow the club to slide through the sand and get the ball high in the air. To get the ball out of the sand, your clubhead will splash through the sand (think of an oar skimming the water) and disperse sand along with your ball. (After you hit your ball out, course etiquette requires that you rake the sand smooth of your footprints and shot.)

When hitting a sand shot, you want the club to go behind the ball and into the sand. Your goal is to leave a spray of sand as your ball flies out of the trap.

132

ASK THE EXPERTS

How hard do I swing?

You don't want to chop at the sand. You want to stay loose so the clubhead can glide through the sand rather than simply dig at it. If the ball is buried in the sand, you need to make a steeper, stronger swing with little follow through.

How do I start to practice hitting balls out of the sand trap?

Most golf courses have a practice sand trap. Get a bucket of balls and your sand wedge. First practice hitting the sand with your sand wedge without the ball. Once you can do that consistently, start swinging really big so that you now splash sand onto the green. Now get out your ball. Your task is to splash the sand onto the green, which in turn will lift the ball onto the green. If you do it right, your club never actually touches the ball.

What is a flop shot?

This is a difficult shot that requires a lob or a sand wedge and enough practice and confidence to take a full swing for a very short shot. You need to practice this at the range before you try it on the golf course. The loft on the club will get the ball high in the air, but you also need the ball sitting up in the grass so you can get under it with a full swing. You'll swing like the shot is going 200 yards, but it will only go 20 yards, flying high and landing softly.

now what do I do?

Answers to common questions

How do I know if I want to pitch or chip and what's the right club to use for these shots?

If the distance to land the ball on the green is a third of the way or less between you and the flagstick, you'll want to use a pitch shot. Use a higher-lofted club such as a pitching wedge, sand wedge, or lob wedge. In a pitch shot, the ball flies farther than it rolls.

If the distance to land the ball on the green is more than a third of the way between you and the flag-stick, use the chip shot. For this you can use any of your mid- to short irons. Some golfers have a favorite chip-ping iron and use it all the time, regardless of the lie or the distance. The key to a good chip shot lies in the swing, not so much the choice of club. Remember: A chips shot rolls farther than it flies.

Sometimes I hit a chip shot and the ball barely moves. Why does that happen?

Golfers have a name for this: the chili dip. You're not far off the green, you dearly want to get the ball close to the hole, but you hit behind the ball with your chip. It moves just a few feet forward and you're heartbroken. First, be aware of the difference between tenacity and tenseness. Worrying about whether the club you selected will provide enough loft can cause you to flip your wrists at impact. Anxiety can also cause you to stop the swing at impact. Keep your arms moving and your left wrist firm. Your weight should be more on your left foot throughout the shot. Grip the club lightly enough so you can feel the shot and keep the club moving at an equal pace in both directions. Finish the same distance as your backswing.

A friend has a club called a chipper. Should I get one?

A chipper is a hybrid club that is somewhere between a putter and a 7-iron. It allows you to feel as if all you're doing is putting the chip and yet has enough loft on the clubface to help the ball get rolling. If it helps you make consistent chip shots, then put it in your bag. No shot will mean more for your score than the chip shot.

I need to improve my swing. What will help?

Consider practicing with a teaching club called a "power fan." This strange-looking contraption forces you to swing with your entire body, not just your arms and legs.

Helpful Resources

BOOKS

Faldo: A Swing for Life
by Nick Faldo

The Long and Short of It
by Andy North

Turning Three Shots into Two: How to Putt, Chip, Pitch, and Blast Your Way to Lower Scores
by Bill Moretti

Chapter 9

The Putt

On the green 138
Assess the green like a pro

Lining up the putt 140
Where does the green break?

The grip and stance 142
There are many ways to go

The right stroke 144
Keep it steady

Controlling distance 146
Don't over-hit the ball

Improving accuracy 148
Tips to help you line up the ball

Now what do I do? 150
Answers to common questions

HOW A PRO
WOULD PLAY IT

Moderate par 4
433 yards

"I'd hit the longest drive possible.
My second shot would be a short
iron because the green is small
and surrounded by three hazards."

on the green

You've finally arrived at the promised land

It's a thrill to walk toward the green and see your ball on the putting surface. Maybe you've hit a mid-iron straight enough or a fairway wood far enough to get there. You've done it! Well, almost—what happens next will likely have more to do with your score than anything else. Among better players, more than 40 percent of their shots are taken on the green. You don't have to be a great athlete to putt the ball. You should relish this part of the game, and get good at it. In walking or riding toward the hole, try to circle past your ball while leaving your clubs or cart at the back of the green nearest the direction of the next tee.

Suggested rules of putting:

1. The ball farthest from the hole is played first.
2. Don't step in anyone's line.
3. Stand still and quiet.
4. Take the flagstick out of the hole or tend it when needed.

Putting Etiquette

Following protocol on the green is a little like standing in line at the deli counter. You need to know when it is your turn. As you walk on the green to **mark your ball**, be aware of the other balls. You don't want to walk on someone's line, the path their ball will take to the hole. So you stay behind their ball and the hole. Marking your ball allows you to clean it and remove it from the green so that it doesn't distract others while they putt.

How do you mark it? You can use a coin or the plastic dime-size ball markers sold or given away in pro shops. Put a marker directly behind your ball. Then lift your ball and replace it when it is your turn to putt. If you are nearest the hole, be prepared to tend the pin, holding it for others if they are so far away they can't see the hole without it. Once the putt is struck, the pin must be removed. The farthest player from the hole putts first. If you putt and hit another ball on the green, you are assessed a two-stroke penalty. So ask that balls be marked if they aren't. If you are off the green and hit another ball on it, there is no penalty. Your ball is played from where it ends up; the other ball is replaced where it was before yours hit it.

The player whose ball is closest to the hole usually gets to **tend the pin** because he or she will be putting last. This means the player has to stand by the flagstick and pick it up whenever someone putts. Why? When on the green, if a player's putt hits the flagstick, it's considered a penalty.

lining up the putt

Putting would be fairly mechanical if every green were absolutely flat. But they weren't flat when sheep were used to keep greens short at the turn of the 20th century, and they aren't flat today after a course designer like Pete Dye gets finished building them. On most newer courses the greens are designed with various slopes that cause putts to **break,** or curve right or left. The amount of break will depend on the steepness of the slope and, of course, the speed of your putt. What will affect the direction of the putt more than anything else is the slope near the hole.

If you aren't putting first, watch other putts and what they do near the hole. Do they break left or right? Stop suddenly? Roll past the hole? You could have those same problems. Observe, learn, and adjust. When it's your turn to putt, pick a spot on the green that you observed another player's ball crossing on its way to the hole. It might be a tiny speck or a slight color change in the grass. Aim for that spot. If you're putting first, and you think there is a break, aim the width of, say, two golf balls to the right or the left. And don't forget about speed, for it will affect the path of the putt as well.

It's a cruel fact but true: Most putting greens have breaks built into them to make sinking your putt that much more of a challenge. To check for breaks, bend down and look closely at the green, note any slight curve or break, and try to compensate for it when you putt.

140

Ways to Putt Well

1. Know your putting speed. Speed control is 90 percent of putting. You need to control the pace of the putter head to control the distance the ball travels.

2. Check your alignment. Put the putter directly behind the ball with the face lined up with where you want the putt to go. Make sure your shoulders are parallel to the line of the putt, and your eyes are looking straight down over the ball. Let your arms hang down directly from your shoulders. Grip the putter lightly so you can feel the stroke and judge the distance.

3. Avoid jerking. Take a smooth, pendulum-type stroke, with your hands, wrists, arms, and shoulders acting as one. Keep your head still and your wrists quiet.

4. Accelerate. Make sure the putter head is accelerating (not slowing down) as you hit the ball. Beginners often take the putter head back so far that in order to control the speed of the putt, they slow down as the putter head approaches the ball. Decelerating causes the putter head to get off line.

5. Practice, practice, practice. It is important to be able to putt from 30 feet and get the ball to within two or three feet of the hole and then, from there, putt it into the hole. Also, practice putting on uphill and downhill lies.

the grip and stance

Find the right grip

There is no end to the many putting grips out there. In the typical full swing grip, the left hand turns slightly to the right, helping to promote the rotation of the clubhead. (See page 98 for more on standard grips.)

Not so in putting. You don't want any rotating of the club when you putt. The hands should be neutral, palms facing each other. The hands are often joined by the use of the reverse-overlapping grip, the index finger of the left hand overlapping the little finger of the right hand. After you've put the face of your putter perpendicular to the line you want to follow, take your stance with your feet parallel to the line. Position your head and eyes over the ball. Get comfortable.

Remember that you cannot rest your club in the sand before you take a shot. You must keep it hovering over the sand, but you can wiggle your feet into the sand to give yourself some traction.

The Left-hand Low Grip for Putting

Some say this is a grip born out of frustration. When all is said and done, it might be the grip for you even before you're frustrated with the more conventional one. Unlike the regular swing where your left hand is above your right, the left-hand low grip (for right-handed golfers) is just what its name suggests. Grip the club with the right hand, and then put the left hand below it. This grip really demands a pendulum motion. It keeps your arms and elbows close to your body. There is no way your right hand can take over as it can with the conventional grip. You aren't as concerned about jerking the putt and thus have less tendency to be tense. Again, this is a tough transformation for someone who has used the conventional grip for years. It might not be so tough for you. With the long putters, the left hand is used to anchor the end of the shaft in the chest or the belly.

FIRST PERSON DISASTER STORY

Mark your ball carefully

I had gotten in the habit of marking my ball by sticking a wooden tee in the ground behind it. The rules allow you to do that, but it's a bad habit. In a tournament, when I pulled the tee from behind my ball, it created a little hole, which my ball rolled right into. This made for a much more difficult putt—I had to play the ball from where it ended up after I replaced it. I learned my lesson: Use a thin coin or a ball marker instead of a tee.

Presley J., Bainbridge Island, Washington

the right stroke

Getting the ball
rolling toward
the hole

Because you are putting on real ground and grass, there will be irregularities that cause the ball to move in unexpected ways. Even the pros only make about half their putts from six feet away.

To putt well, you must keep your head still. If you can, align your eyes directly over the ball and your shoulders parallel to the target line, and then with your shoulders, arms, wrists, and hands acting as one, make a stroke that allows your putter head to stay square through impact. The stroke should go forward as far as it has gone back, allowing for an accelerating motion. A common fault among beginners is to take the club so far back that, in order not to overshoot the hole, they have to slow the club down when it strikes the ball. So pick a line you want your putt to follow, make a confident stroke that sends the ball on its predetermined direction, and realize that the worst thing that can happen is you'll miss.

The key to good putting is an easy, smooth stroke.

ASK THE EXPERTS

How do I keep from getting too nervous when I putt?

Trust is the key. Trust the line you've picked, trust the stroke you've practiced. Taking a deep breath before your putt is also a good idea. Pros fight nerves, or yips as they are called in golf. They check their line; they take a few rehearsal strokes to get a feel for the distance; they put the putter head squarely behind the ball, assume their stance, and pull the trigger. They do this whether on a practice round or the final round of the British Open.

I can't seem to tell whether a putt is uphill or downhill.

You can often be fooled on judging putts. From one angle the putt can appear uphill, from another downhill. Get to the side of the putt as you approach it. The side angle will also help you judge the distance. Don't be reluctant to have someone tend the pin for a long putt. In trying to judge the distance, you will find that the pin and the person tending it will give you some perspective.

controlling distance

The most important aspect in putting

As you strike a putt, the last thing to go through your mind will probably be direction—getting the ball to go where it is aimed. Work to change your last thought so that it is about how well you are going to hit the putt. The distance the ball rolls is important on a number of fronts. Its speed or pace will help determine the direction it rolls on greens that have a discernible slope.

The speed of the putt will also determine where it ends up. From beyond 20 feet, the chances of even the players on the professional tour making a putt are slim—usually 20 percent or less. They want to give their long putt a chance to sneak into the hole, but their goal is more about getting the ball to stop within a foot or two of the cup, giving them an easy next putt. While distance control is vital on long putts, it is also important on a five-foot putt if there is some slope to the green. That's when the speed of your stroke is key. A putt struck softly may move so slowly that it gets caught in a break and goes left or right of the cup. A putt hit with some speed will hopefully glide over any break and drop into the cup.

Developing Feel

It will take practice to develop a sense of how hard to hit a putt. After a while, you will know the second you've struck the ball whether it was hit too hard or too soft—in golf this is called feel. Practice hitting putts with your eyes closed. Another way to promote feel is to imagine as you look at the putt how hard you would have to roll it with an underhand pitching motion.

To hit the putt the distance you want, you need to make good contact with the ball. Your stroke should lengthen as the distance of your putt does, going back farther and coming through farther. When you get to the golf course, allow time to hit some long putts on the practice green, getting a feel for the speed of the grass. Good putters have a good tempo to their stroke; it allows them to translate their feel into action. Think about getting the ball near the hole rather than sinking the putt—that rarely happens. Remember, think speed.

improving accuracy

Worry about the journey, not the destination

As in your other shots, you can't hit the golf ball where you want if you aren't lined up properly. On the practice green, assume a stance parallel to your intended line; then check your alignment by placing one of your other clubs on the ground in front of your feet. Check the line of that club—it will reveal your real line.

To hit straight putts you need to keep your head still, then make a stroke that keeps the head of your putter square at impact. Make sure your backswing and follow through are about the same distance. Putting is stressful. No one wants to miss one, but don't be so results oriented that you worry more about the destination than the journey. Trust your stroke and the line that you've chosen. Don't take undue time over the ball. Thirty seconds is all you should take to read the green, take a practice stroke, and then hit.

On the course, align your putt with the flagstick and check for any breaks on the green.

ASK THE EXPERTS

Where can I practice putting?

Every course has a practice putting green, usually near the first tee. You'll always want to roll a few putts before you play to assess the speed of the greens. Most players spend far more time busting balls on the driving range than they do practicing putting. Half the game is chipping and putting, so practice accordingly.

How should I practice putting?

For some reason, people choose to practice the 6- to 10-foot putts. A better idea is to practice putts from 3 feet and 30 feet, and not so many in between. You want to develop feel on the long putts, both for distance and the effect the green's slope will have on your putt. You want to get the ball to finish up a few feet away from the hole. Then you want to be able to make the next putt, even if your first putt has drifted three or four feet away. Practice the short putt. Practice keeping your head still and making a short, smooth stroke. You need the confidence practice will produce.

now what do I do?

What is a gimme, and should I take one?

Players often concede short putts to their companions in a friendly round of golf. Why bother standing over the ball to make a one-inch or one-foot putt? They give it to you and thus it becomes a **gimme**. The process tends to speed up play and ease frayed nerves, but it can get carried away when putts of three and four feet are conceded. The problem is that your score for handicap purposes becomes somewhat polluted, and you don't develop the skill and confidence necessary to make the three-footer when you really have to. Use this tradition judiciously, if at all.

I've putted to within four feet of the pin. Can I just putt again?

The notion that the person farthest from the hole putts first is generally followed. But once you've made a putt, you have the option of putting again and again until you are in the hole. It helps speed up the game if you just keep putting, but don't be so rushed that you don't take the time to properly line up the putt.

Should I take as much time on the green as the pros do?

No way, José. You want to give yourself a good chance to make a putt, but your livelihood doesn't depend upon it. The key is to check the terrain and get your line while everyone else is doing the same. You can get a feel for the green as you approach your ball from the fairway. You can crouch down behind the ball to determine your line while your companions are putting, even take a few practice strokes to get the feel of the distance. When your turn comes, you're ready.

The long putter looks awkward. Should I really try one?

You won't care what it looks like if it helps you make a few putts. The mechanics surrounding the long putter make sense. You are more likely to make a solid pendulum stroke with the end of the putter shaft anchored to your chest or belly than you are with a conventional putter.

I can't seem to control the directions of my putt. What am I doing wrong?

A common error is to put too much wrist action into a putt. This can put a spin on the ball and send it off in the wrong direction. Don't let your hands get in the way. Consider them an extension of your putter. Your arms and your hands should remain in the same position through the entire putt—no bending of arms or wrists once you start your putt. This will help ensure that the ball is hit from the center (or sweet spot) of your putter, not its heel or tip. You want your putter to hit the ball squarely. Let the movement of your shoulder, not your hands and arms, be the force behind your putter.

Helpful Resources

WEB SITES

www.puttingzone.com
The work of Geoff Mangum, who has a database of 10,000 entries on the art of putting

BOOKS

Dave Pelz's Putting Bible
by Dave Pelz, with James A. Frank
The second in a series of books by a former NASA research analyst on the short game

Putting Out of Your Mind
by Bob J. Rotella

Chapter 10

Improving Your Game

Fixing the slice 154
There is a cure

Fixing the hook 156
Solutions abound

Improper backswing 158
It can ruin a good swing

Hitting too low and too high 160
A common problem

Poor putting 162
Practice makes better

How to practice 164
Try all the shots, not just the drives

Overcoming golf anxiety 166
Find your quiet zone

Mental tips 168
Anxious is as anxious does

Tips to lower your score 170
Very smart things

Competition dos and don'ts 172
Fun with matchplay

Gambling 174
Don't overdo it

Now what do I do? 176
Answers to common questions

HOW A PRO
WOULD PLAY IT

Easy par 3
178 yards

"I'd test for wind direction and adjust my shot accordingly. I wouldn't use a long iron here; it could take the shot over the green."

fixing the slice

Golf's single most frustrating malady

The banana ball, the slice—whatever you want to call it when the ball makes a big bend to the right and loses distance in the process. One of the problems with the slice is that the more you intuitively try to correct it by swinging to the left, the worse things get.

There are two main reasons for the slice. Either the clubface on your club is too open (to the right of square) at impact, or you are swinging to the left and cutting across the ball—something accentuated when you use the driver. To fix the clubface problem, you need to square the clubface by strengthening your grip and turning your left hand more toward the right. Then make sure your swing path is pointed toward the target.

If your swing is causing the problem, don't fret. This is hard to fix by yourself. Consider taking a lesson from a PGA professional.

There are many reasons for a slice. One of the more common problems is a weak grip, which can then cause you to hit the ball with an open or turned clubface instead of a clubface that is parallel to the ball.

ASK THE EXPERTS

Can my setup cause me to slice?

Sure, if your clubface is open at address, if your shoulders are pointed left, and if your stance is too wide and you aren't able to shift your weight to your right side and back to your left. When practicing, put a club in front of your toes and along the target line to see if your shoulders and feet are properly aligned.

I'm set up correctly. Could my backswing be causing the problem?

You need a one-piece takeaway, your shoulders, arms, and hands acting as one. If you jerk the club back during the takeaway instead of gently dragging it back, the path of your swing is likely to be outside in, almost before you get started. A one-piece takeaway (see page 102) should set you on your way to a good swing path.

What should I practice?

Try short swings with the club going back slightly inside and coming naturally back down toward the ball. Rotate your hands. Hit a few hooks off the tees; it will feel good and you'll get the idea of swinging inside out instead of outside in. Place something parallel to the swing and just outside the ball—like a shoebox—to make sure your backswing starts straight down the line.

What is the pull?

This is where the ball does not curve, but flies straight left of your intended target.

fixing the hook

The hook goes farther, but sometimes that's not good

A problem for better players, but still a problem, is the hook. The hook starts a little right but then goes left, way left—it's the opposite of the slice. As legendary golfer Lee Trevino used to say, "You can talk to a slice [asking it to stop], but a hook won't listen." A slight hook is called a draw, which can be a good shot for those who lack distance because the ball rolls farther than normal. The full-fledged hook, however, can go careening out of bounds at the flick of a wrist.

The hook is caused by the clubface being closed at impact and also by the swing path being to the right. Check your alignment and your grip. Are you lining up to the right and not realizing it? Has your grip gotten too strong, with both the left and the right hand turned more to the right than normal, promoting too much rotation of the hands at impact? If you wear a wristwatch on your left wrist, check to see that the face of your watch is pointed to the target line on the backswing.

The hook can be caused by a number of errors, the most common being a closed clubface. Another is improper foot alignment.

ASK THE EXPERTS

How do I stop hooking?

When you're reading about initiating the downswing with a movement of the left hip, be sure you understand the difference between rotating your hips and simply sliding toward the ball. To avoid the slide, make sure you turn your torso during the backswing. If you start sliding toward the ball, your whole swing will get out of synch, and to catch up with your hips your hands will close, causing your clubface to close, resulting in a hook. Also, make sure you're swinging the club straight back instead of too far inside, which creates a swing that is flat, goes right, and eventually closes the clubface. Swing slower, rotate your hips, and make sure your grip has the clubface square at impact.

I want a draw, not a hook. How do I do that?

First, try to eliminate the problems that cause slicing: aiming to the left, too weak a grip, or a move at the start of the downswing that tries to bring the club back outside the natural swing plane. Take the club straight back at the start of your backswing and bring it straight forward while at the same time letting the club release and rotate naturally. This will produce a draw.

What is a push?

Unlike a slice, which starts left and then curves right, a push starts right and stays right.

improper backswing

When the
takeaway isn't
slow and low

Because you hit the ball on your downswing you could deduce that the backswing has nothing to do with hitting the ball. Bad deduction. The backswing is vitally important. It gets you in a proper position to hit the ball, and it can also establish the tempo that will be repeated during the downswing. The key is a one-piece takeaway, the hands, arms, and shoulders moving as one. Or, as most teachers describe it, slow and low.

Beginners tend to swing as if they were taking the club back primarily with their right hand, a lifting motion rather than a smooth dragging one. (See page 102 for more on the takeaway.) This causes the arc of the swing to diminish and the left arm to bend radically, reducing the amount of power you can develop and causing various other problems along the way. You want to sweep the ball low, with the left arm and the club extended but not rigid. The club needs to rotate with your body. By the time the club is parallel to the ground, your wrists have cocked or set. From there, simply continue to turn until your left shoulder has grazed your chin.

ASK THE EXPERTS

I think my body sways back as I start the backswing. Is that right?

Your body rotates; it doesn't sway. Keep your good posture at address, the knees slightly bent, your spine straight, your shoulders level, and then turn, the stomach moving with the hands, arms, and shoulders in the one-piece takeaway.

Is there a drill I can practice to get the feel of this torso turn?

A lot of teaching pros talk about this one. Take a normal stance with a 5-iron. Grip way down on the shaft of the club, or far enough that the end of the shaft comes to rest at your belly button. From there start your backswing, and rotate until the point at which your wrists start to cock, about 8 o'clock. This will help you develop the sensation of the body rotating with the club. Do it again and again.

I'd like some checkpoints for a good backswing.

In his book *How I Play Golf*, Tiger Woods gives you six things to check at the top of your backswing: The left shoulder is turned under the chin, the clubface is square or parallel to the left forearm, the left heel is flat, weight has gathered on the right foot, the right knee is flexed, and the right elbow points at the ground.

hitting too low and too high

Trying to fix shots that are fat, thin, and in the sky

A poorly hit shot that goes low and not very far is often said to have been hit **fat**, meaning you hit the ground before you hit the ball. Simply having the ball back too far and then subconsciously trying to slide forward with your hips to hit it can cause a fat shot. It can also happen if your grip pressure is too tight. Another cause is a maneuver called the **reverse pivot**, where your weight, instead of moving to your right foot on the backswing, moves to your left foot. Then as you swing down at the ball, the weight shifts back to your right foot.

The solution also lies with correct ball positioning—or where your feet are in relation to the ball. Ideally, when you hit a drive, the ball is positioned in between your feet. But what can happen is that you unconsciously move your feet when you officially address the ball. You think the ball is in the middle of your stance, but your feet have moved well back of that. Ball position can have a lot to do with hitting the ball too high or too low. Often, the ball played too far forward will be hit on the upswing and go too high; one played back too far might never get off the ground.

When using the driver, align the ball with the instep of your left foot. The ball should be teed up so that the top of your driver comes to the middle of the golf ball.

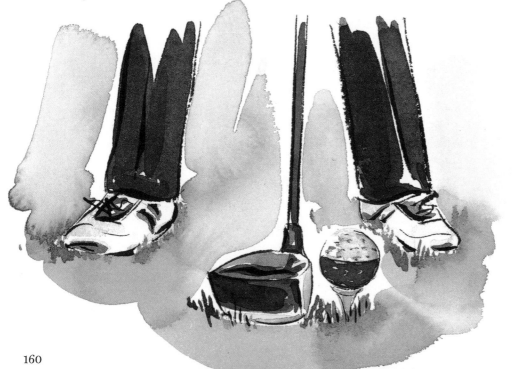

ASK THE EXPERTS

I keep hitting the upper part of the golf ball. What can I do about it?

This is called **topping the ball**, and it happens to a lot of beginning golfers. There are a number of things to consider here. Your grip might be too tight, your knees might have lost their flex, or you might be losing your balance in the swing. Try to turn your hips, not slide them, on the backswing. You want the weight on your right side, not your left, on the backswing. Otherwise you get the dreaded reverse pivot, and a top.

What happens when I "sky the ball" off the tee?

A sky ball is a ball that goes very high up in the air, but not very far down the fairway. It means you've swung underneath the ball. You are taking the club up sharply and bringing it down sharply. Your grip might be too strong (the left hand over too far to the right), or you might be standing too close to the ball, even too upright. Make a full, smooth turn, and don't jump at the ball when you're trying to hit it.

poor putting

When the ball doesn't
go near, or in, the hole

You want putting to help you make up strokes, not lose them. Remember, more than 40 percent of the strokes you'll take in a round are on the putting green. So don't overlook this aspect of the game when you're practicing, especially the day you play. Roll some long putts on the practice green, and build some confidence in your ability to get the ball near the hole. Get a feeling of the speed of the greens.

Nothing helps your putting more than the confidence that comes with understanding the pace of the putts and knowing you can make the three-footer. Practice long putts and short putts, remembering, of course, the basic fundamentals of putting. Stay steady, don't move your head to see where the putt is going, and accelerate the clubhead through impact. Remember that you want your stroke to be the same length on the follow through as on the backswing. Practice making good contact and hitting the ball on your putter's sweet spot.

ASK THE EXPERTS

I miss short putts. Do I have the yips?

Let's hope not. The **yips** are a nervous reaction to the fear of missing a short putt. Fear interferes with the process, and you get a terrible jerk instead of a stroke. Have fun, don't worry. Everyone misses short putts, even the pros. The short putt is an easier version of the long one. Use the same technique. Trust the line you've picked. Worry about keeping your head still instead of missing the putt.

What else do I need to know about making short putts?

If you're missing many of them, check your alignment. It is possible you are aligned either to the right or left of the hole and do not know it. The anxiety involved with the short putt may also cause you to speed up. Don't vary your routine. Take a practice swing to understand the speed of the putt, stay steady, take a deliberate backswing, and then accelerate through impact. Think about making the putt, not missing it.

What is a three-jack?

That's the three-putt green, something you hope to avoid. Everyone three-putts on occasion. To have as few as possible, the goal on the green should not be to make every single putt. The goal should be to take no more than two putts. Relax and get the feeling for the green and how it breaks.

how to practice

**It's all a matter
of priority**

As much as people talk about their desire to lower their score, much of the joy in golf comes from hitting the ball high and far. So it is that most golfers go to the practice range, warm up hitting a few wedge shots, and then pound 50 or 60 shots with their driver. Professionals practice all their shots equally. They practice to get loose and to identify any problem tendencies at the moment.

So, do what the pros do. Practice all types of shots, and notice any problems. If you are hitting most of your shots to the right, it's safe to assume you will do the same on the golf course. Take care of the problem while you are practicing. Check your stance, your ball position, your grip. A lot of golfers try to find their swing while they take their practice swings on the first tee. That's too late. Try to hit some practice balls before you play.

For regular practice at the driving range, start with a review of the fundamentals. Check your grip, your stance, the ball position, and most importantly, your alignment. Put a club on the ground to check your alignment. Next, make sure you hit all the different types of shots, from the drive to the sand shot. Your goal is to achieve what golfers call **muscle memory**, where your body innately recalls the proper muscle motion needed for each shot.

ASK THE  EXPERTS

I hear people talk about practicing the way you play. What does that mean?

After you work on fundamentals, play the course on the range. Hit a tee shot, then an approach shot. Find a target. Concentrate on it. This will help you make the shot on the course when you have to. If you can, practice hitting uphill, downhill, and side-hill lies. Practice hitting out of the rough, out of the sand. You'll develop not only technique, but confidence.

Is it possible I'm swinging too hard on the range?

Everybody wants to hit the ball far. Subconsciously you swing harder and harder. One reason is that here you don't really care where the ball goes, but on the course you will. Work on a specific aspect of the swing, like better rotation of the clubhead, and don't just correct the mistake made on the last shot you hit. Constant correcting only confuses your brain.

Can I practice my short game at the range?

Sure you can, even if there isn't an area devoted to it. Practice what the pros call the half shot, the 50-yard wedge shot. The half shot requires body turn and acceleration even though you don't want the ball to go very far. The half shot will eventually help your fundamentals with the full shot, and it will help you lower your score.

overcoming golf anxiety

Remember, it's just a game

Neither the golfers in your group nor the other players on the course will be focused on the results of your first tee shot. And no matter what happens, the experience won't be life-threatening. Everyone is going to be nervous on the first tee. At some point everyone has a terrible shot or two or three.

Your confidence will be directly related to your amount of preparation. Did you get to the course early enough to warm up? Did you take care of the little things: enough balls in your bag, a ball marker, tees, that sort of thing. Okay, now it is time to focus on where you are trying to go and how you are going to get there.

Good players say they don't think about the mechanics of their swing during a round. Instead they try to visualize the path of the ball. You do the same. Pick a target to visualize reaching and then imagine the flight of the ball as it goes in that direction.

If you get nervous, give yourself a set of steps, like washing the ball and fixing your glove. Do them in order before you tee off.

ASK THE EXPERTS

Why do I always seem to hit the ball into the water rather than over it?

You're seeing the ball go into the water and not over it. So you either hit behind the ball, or in trying not to hit behind it, you top it. Forget the water. Hit the ball squarely at a cloud.

How do I learn to get over bad shots?

Bad shots can build up a layer of mental scar tissue, so try to remember the good shots you've hit with a particular club or on a particular hole, not the bad ones. Focus on making a smooth and slow swing with good solid contact.

FIRST PERSON DISASTER STORY

No hero here

It's called the hero shot—that's where a player forgoes the easy shot for the really difficult one. I had always wanted to try one and I finally got a chance while playing with a friend on his course. He lived in Arizona, and the course had a canyon on its par 5. Wow. There's nothing like hitting a shot over a canyon onto the green, eschewing the easy shot. Unfortunately, the Arizona canyon proved not to be a problem because I never made it there. A tall saguaro cactus got in the way—my ball got embedded high in the cactus. It helped that it was not the first one to get stuck there. It was peppered with balls. I had to replay the shot, hitting three. Sometimes the heroic thing to do is the sensible thing.

Jackson L., Chicago, Illinois

mental tips

When and when not to think

It is interesting how often you'll do a better job executing a difficult shot than an easy one, specifically one that requires getting out of trouble. You walk up to the shot and try to visualize the various paths the ball can take: under a tree, over a ditch, onto a green that is very firm. You let your creative side take over, putting aside for a moment all the mechanical thoughts of how to make this shot. The pros do that same kind of thinking on all their shots. They see it, feel it, and think more about the destination than the journey.

John Brodie, the famous football quarterback who later became a member of the PGA Senior Tour, was asked what was easier, football or golf? He didn't hesitate. "Football, because all you have to do is react," he said. "The golf ball doesn't move, and you've got too much time to think about things." You never hear a quarterback talk about the mechanics of passing, or a pitcher about how he throws the ball. Practice when it is time to practice, and play when it is time to play.

Start visualizing your shot from the moment you select a club—it's a good way to keep focused.

168

ASK THE EXPERTS

What should I think about when I swing?

The last thing you look at before looking at the ball should be the target. You can visualize a green in the fairway to help you focus better. After that, think about tempo, not mechanics. Imagine the golf swing as a dance step. Pretend you're waltzing, or visualize whatever you can in order to get some rhythm in what you're doing.

Is the target always the pin?

It depends on the shot you are taking. Use some strategy, especially off the tee when faced with dog-legs to the left or right. In those cases, you might need to hit to the right or left of the pin and then work your way to a straighter target. Also, check the wind—it can pull a straight shot left or right.

A dog-leg hole is a good example of how the target is not always the pin. In a dog-leg you often cannot see the pin from the tee.

tips to lower your score

Decide what you
need to work on

You must be honest here. Do you want to lower your score or do you just want to hit the golf ball farther and better? It is understandable that your greatest joy comes from hitting a soaring tee shot. But accept the fact that if you spend all your practice time hitting the drive, you really aren't likely to cut many strokes off your score.

The answer is short game, short game, short game. The object is to have one-putt greens, not three-putt greens. Think about the difference that would make in your score. And realize that this goal is not something that requires great strength or athleticism. Chipping and putting, that's what it requires. You're not going to hit many greens from the tees. The ability to chip the ball onto the green and close enough to make a putt could easily knock 10 shots off your score. Practice chipping, practice long putts near the hole, and practice making short putts.

It can't be said often enough: Practice your short game. There are clubs and driving ranges where you can practice your short irons.

ASK THE EXPERTS

What about when I am out on the course?

Try to play to your strengths. If you can hit a pitching wedge onto the green with pretty fair regularity, then try to get in that position. The alternative from 220 yards out is to try to slam a 3-wood onto the green. Play a 7-iron shot to 100 yards, and hit your wedge. You avoid hitting the 3-wood out of bounds or rolling it into a greenside bunker. If the hole requires three shots for you to get onto the green, divide up the distance and use your most reliable clubs to cover it. Plan conservatively. Ask yourself what your realistic chances are of hitting the ball well enough and far enough to get over a lake in front of the green. Or of threading a shot between two big trees to get onto a green, when a simple pitch-out to the fairway might be the better option. Miracle shots are fun to attempt, but they are called miracles for a reason. While you should plan conservatively, don't get so tentative that you swing the same way. Plan conservatively, swing aggressively. Concentrate on executing whatever shot you've selected. If you find yourself in deep trouble, cut your losses. Get the ball back in the fairway. Be confident you'll make up lost strokes with the chipping and putting you've been practicing, not with some shot you could hit once a millennium.

competition dos and don'ts

For most of the informal competition you find yourself involved in, the format will be some sort of **matchplay**, meaning the result of each hole is more important than the final score. These competitions go by many different names, such as Nassau and scramble (see page 68). Playing matchplay is fun. If you have a bad hole, you just move on to the next one. It is important in golf to stay in the moment, to concentrate on the shot at hand, forgetting about the bad shot you've just made or the bad hole that ruined what promised to be a career round.

Matchplay rewards the ability to concentrate on playing one shot at a time. Rather than playing the course, you are playing your opponent. It can seem that you're hopelessly out of the hole because you've hit your drive into the woods and can only chip back to the fairway, but who is to say your opponent won't have similar problems? Your opponent can be on the green in two shots, and you're just off it in three shots. You get "up and down," making a good chip and a putt, and your opponent takes three putts. You've tied the hole and move on to the next one.

Here's an example of what not to do: Don't stand behind a putter and offer tips. It's distracting, to say the very least.

Matchplay Dos

Do finish "putting out" if you can.

Do strive to keep your ball in play; this puts pressure on your opponent. That might mean hitting a 3-wood or an iron off the tee. On the other hand, if you try to power a big drive and end up out of bounds, or in the rough, or behind a tree, the pressure is on you instead.

Matchplay Don'ts

Don't ever give up. The hole or the round can appear lost, but you never know what your opponent might do. Or what you might do, like sink a 30-footer. The pros call it grinding. You take it one shot, one hole at a time.

Don't get psyched out by either the difficulty of the course or the ability of your opponent. Believe in the handicap system. If your opponent is a 10 handicapper and you're a 20, don't think you're outclassed. The strokes you'll get will be important; they are designed to put you on an equal footing with your opponent. It only works if you feel equal.

Don't try a shot you haven't practiced. Don't let your ego dictate the club you use. When you get into trouble, don't rush into a shot just to get it over with. Slow down.

gambling

A good or bad thing on the course?

On the first tee, you're already anxious about the round, and then someone adds to it by asking, "What are we playing for?" Your heart sinks. Now a bad game will cost you money as well as self-esteem. You want out of there. The truth is the betting isn't as much about money as it is about competition. And, more significantly, concentration. Betting a few dollars on a round will keep you involved in a hole when things seem otherwise hopeless.

A number of match games lend themselves to betting. The most popular match game is a Nassau. Here the winner of the front nine gets a point, the winner of the back nine gets a point and the winner of the whole round gets a point. A normal bet is $2 a point. So the player who wins the front and back nines and thus the whole round wins $6.00. A $2 Nassau can, of course, become a $200 Nassau. That's when you should get anxious. Naw, that's when you shouldn't play.

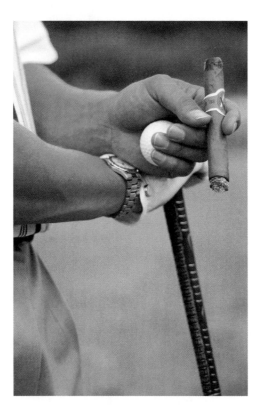

ASK THE EXPERTS

I hear people talking about specials. What are they?

In any game, you can win additional credit—or money—for making special shots, such as a sandy, which means you got out of a sand trap to make a par. There are also specials for being closest to the hole on a par 3. Usually, you lose the point if you two-putt for a par. In a $2 Nassau, specials are normally worth 25 cents.

How do you keep the bad feelings out of betting?

One custom that works nicely is to make an agreement before the game begins that the winners will buy the losers soft drinks or sandwiches after the round, to celebrate the day, and their winnings, of course. Often one drink can equal the amount lost.

FIRST PERSON DISASTER STORY

Golf is a well-rounded game

In some respects, the driving range can be more fun than the golf course. There are no bad shots, just the ones you choose to ignore and try again. I know I was supposed to be practicing to get better on the course, but the fun thing was seeing how far I could hit that tee shot. So I started swinging harder and harder and faster and faster. I ignored the irons altogether and never even bothered trying out a chip shot or two. When I finally got to play on a course, I was so wild, my short game was anything but. I couldn't hit a chip shot anywhere near the green—they kept sailing past, long past. I finally gave up and went back to the driving range and practiced all the shots. Golf is a game that calls for all sorts of swings, clubs, and skills. The smart golfer practices them all.

Dee S., Little Rock, Arkansas

now what do I do?

Answers to
common questions

I think I've got paralysis by analysis. How do I get rid of it?

You've got to remember that golf is an athletic event. Find the target, swing the club, and move on. Try not to go to bat—or the first tee—with more than one swing thought in mind. And don't try to change things after every bad shot. Take a few good practice swings using the basics, and play on.

Give me one best thought about curing my slice.

Try this drill: Separate your hands by four or five inches on the club, and swing slowly, gradually picking up speed, and feel the clubface rotate.

Should I buy new clubs or pay for a series of lessons?

The modern clubs are easier to hit than the old ones. But once you've got perimeter-weighted irons and up-to-date woods, next year's model may not help you as much as manufacturers suggest in their ads. Ongoing instruction coupled with practice is more likely to help you than the search for the perfect putter or driver.

How can I keep from having one really bad hole that ruins my score?

One consoling thought is that the big number, as a bad hole is called, does not really affect your handicap. That's because there is a limit to the score you can report, a seven for those with a handicap less than 20, and an eight or nine for a handicap above 20. But no one wants a 10 or a 12. The key is not making things worse. When you get into trouble, slow down, think about the best way to get back on track, and take it. Don't quit thinking, don't quit trying. Don't try to make it all up by making one shot you've never even tried before, let alone practiced. Take a deep breath and get back to the basics.

I hate the first tee. Can I take a mulligan?

The first tee bothers everyone. The reality is no one cares as much about your first shot as you do. So if you hit it badly or out of bounds, don't fret—everyone has done that before. Taking a **mulligan** is one way to handle the problem. It just means you ask for a do-over and hit a new ball. The first bad shot is simply forgiven. Obviously, mulligans are not allowed in any official game of golf, but in a game among friends they are often done. Some pros caution against taking mulligans. They want you to get up there with the idea that you're going to hit the best shot possible—with no second chances—and move on.

Helpful Resources

WEB SITES

worldgolf.com
A Web site with lots of tips from professionals

BOOKS

David Leadbetter's Faults and Fixes: How to Correct the 80 Most Common Problems in Golf
by David Leadbetter

My Golden Lessons: 100-Plus Ways to Improve Your Shots, Lower Your Scores and Enjoy Golf Much, Much More
by Jack Nicklaus
More than 120 time-tested tips from golf's most decorated player

Zen Golf: Mastering the Mental Game
by Dr. Joseph Par

Chapter 11

Fitting Golf In

Golf on the road 180
You can always find a driving range

Business golf 182
Learn about your players before you deal

Golf vacations 184
Don't forget to include everyone

Irish and Scottish courses 186
Where the game was born

Teaching kids 188
Don't force them

Now what do I do? 190
Answers to common questions

HOW A PRO
WOULD PLAY IT

**Moderate par 4
383 yards**

"I'd hit my drive down the left
side of the fairway. The green is
narrow, so I'd use a 9-iron for a
more accurate second shot."

Golf on the road

Finding practice ranges

You'll know you're hooked on golf when the first thing you look up in the yellow pages of your hotel's phone book is driving ranges, and not restaurants. You'll develop a knack for spotting driving ranges as you drive into town from the airport, the high, dark netting a dead giveaway. Most courses have driving ranges, of course, and usually say so in their yellow pages ads. If you brought your laptop, use the Internet and see what ranges are near you. Or ask at the hotel desk. Surely you aren't the first person looking for one.

Assuming that you didn't bring your clubs with you, the driving range will almost always have clubs you can borrow or rent. They won't be great, and certainly not like yours, but they'll do. As far as playing golf, don't overlook the power of the single, as the lone golfer is called. Drive up, sign up on the singles list, rent some clubs if you don't have them, and in most cases, you'll be on the course playing in 15 or 20 minutes. Golfers assume their twosome or threesome will be filled out by the course management. You'll end up playing with a couple from Topeka or three brokers from Chicago and having a great time.

Taking Your Clubs

By nature, golf clubs are cumbersome. The golf industry has provided a variety of travel bags to transport them. Various airlines, however, are beginning to ask travelers to waive the airline's responsibility should damage occur to clubs not packed in a hard case. The soft travel bags are easier to store and usually cheaper to own. Experienced golfers and travelers often wrap towels around the heads of their metal woods if they use a soft bag. Some put a broom handle or dowel in the bag that is longer than the longest club to protect graphite shafts. Others turn the metal woods over, putting the heads deep in the bag. The traveling case can also be used to contain extra shoes, sweaters, rain gear, even underwear, reducing the load in other suitcases while padding the golf bag. The newer travel bags have wheels that make them easier to drag through airports. Space, however, becomes the problem when three or four of you share a rental car. In that case, rent an SUV or a van.

More airlines are now requiring that you use a hard case as a golf travel bag. You can still use soft bags for local travel but may have to sign a no-fault waiver or pay extra for a special service.

Business golf

Golf lets you combine business with pleasure

The concept of the golf course as a picturesque replacement for the board room in American business is as far off-line as a hooked ball. Businessmen and women do play golf. Clients do get to know one another on the course. But anyone who loves golf and cherishes a few hours each week on the course does not want it cluttered with negotiating contracts. Or to be jarred by cell phones in the middle of their backswings.

On the other hand, you can learn a lot about people during a round of golf—about their competitiveness, their composure, their character. Do they cheat? Have they boned up on golf's rules and etiquette? Do they applaud other shots? Add to rather than subtract from the enjoyment of the round? Do they get so lost in the problems they are having that they forget those around them? Do they gamble too much, talk too much, or drink too much? After four hours, without conducting any business at all, you're likely to know a lot about the people you played with.

Some Business Golf Dos and Don'ts

Don't bring a cell phone to the course.

The cell phone is an unwanted and unwarranted addition to the golf course. It shatters the mood of the day, the concentration needed for a shot, and the golfer's code of conduct. Better that someone come out to the course to get you in case of an emergency.

Don't whine about your game.

Nobody has enough time to play or practice, so don't even bring it up. Everyone has hit horrible shots. You won't be special in that regard. You won't be judged by how bad a shot you hit, but by how you handle it. Throwing clubs and kicking bags is reprehensible, not to mention dangerous. And what does it say about your composure? So hit the ball, and go hit it again, happy just to be playing golf.

Do brush up on etiquette and rules.

Call the course and see what attire is acceptable, including whether you need soft spikes in your shoes. Have the necessary items to play a round: balls, tees, ball markers. Do something as simple as counting the number of clubs in your bag to make sure there aren't more than 14.

Golf vacations

Making room for the interests of others

There are golf vacations, and there are golf vacations. Assuming you will take your significant other along, or even kids if you have them, you need to think about what else there is to do in the day—and the night—besides play golf. Golf junkets are easy to put together. Money can be saved by booking the golf and accommodations in a package deal, paying a daily, or weekly, rate that provides a single charge for both.

Consider your partner's needs as well as your own. For many, golf is just a sidelight, so the accommodations are important. Is there a pool, a nice dining room, shopping nearby? This might not be vital to you, but it can be for those with you. (Resort golf courses offer a lot of other sporting activities; see page 32.)

If your partner loves the game as much as you, but plays at a different level, find out how difficult the course is where you might be staying. Check and see how crowded the course might be at that time of year. Some husbands and wives prefer playing as a twosome on vacations. If that is important to you, pick an off-season time when the course isn't likely to be busy. Conversely, if you welcome being assigned another twosome in order to play, then the busy seasons should do just fine.

The resort at Squaw Creek in Lake Tahoe, California, offers something for everyone—swimming, golf, skiing, and a first-class spa.

How to Set Up a Golf Vacation

Consider a place like Myrtle Beach, South Carolina, where there are more than 100 golf courses on a stretch of coast. Package deals are endless, priced according to the quality of the course and the accommodations. At Myrtle Beach, golf is cheaper in the summer when it is very hot, but accommodations are more expensive then because you are competing with the summer vacation crowd. Golf is always cheaper in the off-season. Golf courses in Arizona are half the price in June that they are in January. Northeast coast golf courses are in high demand in June but not January. Hawaii is always expensive. There are wonderful places to go that aren't, from Okanagan, British Columbia, to the Robert Trent Jones Trail in Alabama. Some people prefer Pinehurst to Pebble Beach; most can't afford either. If you love golf, you can find a course to suit you. Just remember that there are a few other factors to consider, since most likely you won't be playing golf every day.

Irish and Scottish courses

Playing where golf is all there is

Exotic usually means Hawaii or New Zealand, or something along those tropical lines. But to a real golfer, exotic means playing golf where it all began, in Scotland or its exciting neighbor, Ireland. This becomes a different type of golf vacation, where golf can be all you do, and usually is. You travel across the Atlantic to a place where the course conditions aren't particularly good and the weather is even worse. There are few if any golf carts, and the pace of play is as steady and unrelenting as the winds coming off the North Atlantic. This is about playing **links** golf, on land virtually reclaimed from the sea, land without trees; sandy, pockmarked,

wind-swept land. The beauty is that everything is natural—the courses, the people, and the game. You recover from a day of wind and rain with a pint of Guinness or a glass of single malt scotch. You play courses where they play the British Open. You play golf the way it was meant to be played.

If you want to try your hand at a serious links course, there is nothing finer than the Old Course at St. Andrews in Scotland.

ASK THE EXPERTS

How difficult are the courses in Scotland and Ireland?

With the wind up, they can be almost impossible. Often you have to "carry" 170 yards of sand, heather, and gorse just to get to the fairway. Those with handicaps of more than 20 will struggle. On the other hand, the ball rolls forever on the hard fairways.

Do I need reservations to play there?

For the courses, yes, but for accommodations, not really. Every other house in Ireland is a bed-and-breakfast. Except for the half dozen famous courses in each country, greens fees are reasonable, from $20 to $40. Once you are there, a golf outing becomes very affordable. Rooms in a straightforward bed-and-breakfast are $50 to $60. They can be shared.

Can I put together a trip myself?

Absolutely. The Internet works well for making golf reservations. Start with something as simple as a search for "golf in Ireland." Make reservations for golf, and figure you'll find available bed-and-breakfasts. Rent a car or a small van, and take off for a golf vacation that is more reasonable and exciting than one in Arizona or Hawaii.

Is there golf in other countries?

Golf is a worldwide sport. All across Europe there are courses, especially in France, Spain, Italy, and Sweden. Golf is very popular in Asia. New Zealand and Australia are dotted with affordable, challenging courses, and their summer is a Northern Hemisphere winter.

Should I go see a professional tournament?

Yes. The PGA, LPGA, and Seniors play tournaments all over the country. It is not only fun, but you can learn a lot by watching the pros in action.

Teaching kids

Show them the game, but don't force it

Golf is serious; kids usually aren't. While golf can be a wonderful game for kids, there's a danger in turning kids off to golf if you push too hard, and they may never embrace it again. Want to get your kids interested in golf? Let them ride in the golf cart or throw rocks in the pond by the No. 7 green. Or knock a plastic whiffle ball around the yard or the house. They don't need to be burdened with heavy clubs and heavy expectations. Clubs are being made these days that actually fit kids, short enough and light enough to be swung with fun, and some success. Kids need the game to be playful, not complicated. More than one teacher has suggested that until they're 12 all the advice they need is about a decent grip, a decent weight shift, and a decent follow through. When they need more they'll ask for it. In the meantime, create fun, competitive situations for your kids so that golf is more a game than an art.

FIRST PERSON DISASTER STORY

I was supposed to be a golf pro

It was all my father ever wanted me to be: a golf pro. He was an avid golfer, and I was daddy's little girl who happened to be a good athlete. It started when I was seven—I remember riding around in his golf cart, reading comics to try to pass the time. Then came the lessons, practice after school. Then golf camp. I did it for my dad, but after a while it was too much. I never got a chance to see if I liked the game for myself. When I was 15, I quit the game. My dad was upset, but he got over it. When it came time to apply to college, I found out that there were many golf scholarships available for women at really top schools. I kind of wish I had stayed with the game. Who knows where it would have led?

Claire T., Santa Monica, California

Golf Camps

Golf can be good for kids. The sport teaches kids to be accountable, not only for their own score and equipment, but for themselves. There are few outside agents on which to blame a poor shot. They learn about taking care of the golf course and being fair and courteous to other players. Golf camps are clinics for kids where an instructor makes learning the basic rules and etiquette of the game so fun, kids don't even realize they're being taught. The youngest age for such camps is usually about seven. Instruction is done in groups. Golf camps or clinics are offered at most courses and golf clubs. An organization called The First Tee is found in many cities. It teaches golf to kids who don't have the resources to get involved in the sport on their own.

now what do I do?

I'm in Cleveland on business. How do I find a game?

Ask the concierge about nearby golf courses and for a printed golf directory. Or open up the phone book to the yellow pages. Call a nearby course and say you want to play as a single. They'll often pair you up with someone. You can even walk up to the course and put your name on the singles list.

Are there any Scottish-type golf courses in the United States?

There are a few. One is Bandon Dunes, located on the south coast of Oregon, where two exceptional links courses have been built on sand dunes reminiscent of those in Ireland and Scotland. The golf here is back-to-basics. No carts, no pampering—just golf.

If I don't take my clubs, can I rent a set?

Most resort courses offer a selection of rental clubs, usually of high quality. Lower-end courses often have lower-end clubs; sometimes you'll even find a real wood in the bag, not a metal one. Pack golf balls, a glove, and shoes if you think you're going to play. Balls are expensive at resort courses, and they don't rent shoes the way they do at bowling alleys.

I'm working on a project that requires me to be on call every day of the week. Can I play golf and keep my cell phone on?

It's best not to play if you have to be in constant communication with work. That said, you can play a round of golf if you exercise cell phone etiquette. Use it only for outgoing calls. Keep it turned off during the round, and check for messages at the end of nine holes or if you end up waiting for long periods of time on the tee. But remember, nobody wants to play with someone who's off in the bushes talking business, or to hear the phone ring in the middle of their backswing.

Helpful Resources

WEB SITES

www.Golfvacations.com
Specializing in U.S. golf outings

www.sghgolf.com
Golf vacation deals worldwide

www.worldgolf.com
Golf destinations around the world

www.randa.org
Official St. Andrews Golf Club home page

BOOKS

A Wee Nip at the 19th Hole: A History of the St. Andrews Caddie
by Richard MacKenzie

500 World's Greatest Golf Holes
by George Peper

Zagat Survey of America's Top Golf Courses

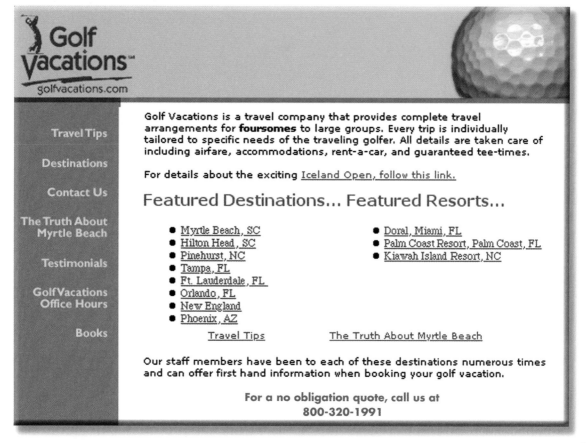

Golf Vacations is a travel company that provides complete travel arrangements for **foursomes** to large groups. Every trip is individually tailored to specific needs of the traveling golfer. All details are taken care of including airfare, accommodations, rent-a-car, and guaranteed tee-times.

For details about the exciting Iceland Open, follow this link.

Featured Destinations... Featured Resorts...

Travel Tips

Destinations

Contact Us

The Truth About Myrtle Beach

Testimonials

Golf Vacations Office Hours

Books

- Myrtle Beach, SC
- Hilton Head, SC
- Pinehurst, NC
- Tampa, FL
- Ft. Lauderdale, FL
- Orlando, FL
- New England
- Phoenix, AZ

- Doral, Miami, FL
- Palm Coast Resort, Palm Coast, FL
- Kiawah Island Resort, NC

Travel Tips   The Truth About Myrtle Beach

Our staff members have been to each of these destinations numerous times and can offer first hand information when booking your golf vacation.

**For a no obligation quote, call us at
800-320-1991**

glossary

Alignment
The position of the body in relation to the target.

Approach shot
The shot that gets you onto the green, normally an iron shot that goes high and lands softly.

Ball marker
A coin or round plastic piece the size of a dime that is placed behind a ball on the green to mark the ball while it is picked up and cleaned.

Ball position
The spot the ball is placed in relation to your feet, forward meaning more toward the left foot, back meaning toward the right.

Birdie
The score of one less than par on a hole, which is the score an expert player is supposed to make.

Bogey
The score of one more than par on a hole. A double bogey is two more, a triple bogey three more.

Bunker
A hole in the ground filled with sand, also called a sand trap. Since it is a hazard, you cannot ground your club while attempting a shot.

Chip shot
A short shot to get you onto the green and close to the hole. The ball usually runs along the ground and is hit with a short or mid-iron.

Closed
Describes the position of the clubface in relation to the ball. If the clubface has gone past square as it strikes the ball, then it is closed. The opposite of open.

Cup

The metal holder for the hole in the green that serves as the final destination for the ball on every hole.

Divot

The clump of grass and dirt that flies out of the ground following a shot with an iron. The divot needs to be replaced if possible.

Dog-leg

A hole that angles sharply to the right or to the left, in a shape that resembles a dog's hind leg.

Draw

A shot hit slightly from right to left, somewhere between straight and a hook.

Driver

The lightest and longest of the clubs, a metal club whose head is often made of titanium, and carries a loft of between 8 and 12 degrees, hitting the ball farther than any other club.

Fade

A shot hit slightly from left to right, somewhere between straight and a slice.

Fairway

The closely mowed grass down the middle of a hole, connecting the teeing area with the green.

Fairway woods

Metal woods used off the fairway, usually numbered 3, 4, 5, and 7. They have more loft than the driver and hit the ball higher.

Fat

The shot that is hit heavy, or behind the ball, meaning the ground is struck first. This shot usually doesn't go very far.

Feel

Around the green, the ability to estimate just how hard a shot needs to be struck, and then doing so. Also called touch.

Flagstick

Also called the pin; this is the long pole with the flag on top of it that sits in the cup of each hole on each green.

Fluff

The same as fat.

Gimme

A putt so short that other players don't make you take it, allowing you to pick up the ball. This saves time and spares you the possibility of missing the shot.

Green

The putting surface at the end of each hole.

Greens fees

The charge for playing a round of golf, usually paid in the pro shop. Fees are often for 9 holes and 18 holes.

Hook

This is a shot that starts to the right and then bends rather dramatically to the left. Opposite of a slice.

Irons

The clubs designated 1 through 9 that are used to hit the ball from the fairway onto the green, 1 having the least loft and 9 the most.

Line

The path or direction the ball must take to get to the hole or wherever the shot is aimed.

Lob wedge

The most lofted of the wedges, usually about 60 degrees, this creates very high shots to the green with little roll.

Loft

The angle of the clubface, measured in degrees, a driver being about 10 degrees, a wedge about 50 degrees, with all the other clubs in between.

Matchplay

A form of competition between two players that is decided by the winner of each hole.

Medal play

A form of competition among players that is decided by the total number of strokes used.

Metal woods

Golf's oxymoron. Driver and fairway woods that used to be made of persimmon wood are now made of high-tech metals—thus the name.

Nassau

A popular, Saturday-morning matchplay competition where points are awarded for winning the front nine, back nine, and the overall 18 holes.

Open

Describes the position of the clubface in relation to the ball. If the clubface has not reached square with the ball, then it is open. The opposite of closed.

Par

The score an expert player is expected to make on each hole. Most courses have ten par 4s, four par 3s, and four par 5s.

Penalty stroke

A penalty stroke is added to your score when your shot goes out of bounds or into a water hazard, or is lost or declared unplayable.

Perimeter-weighted

The modern iron has more weight around the perimeter of its face, making for a bigger "sweet spot" and so more well-struck shots.

Pitching wedge

A club used to make short, high shots to the green, usually with a loft of 48 to 55 degrees.

Pitch shot

A play around the greens that differs from a chip shot in that it goes higher, sometimes farther, and lands softer.

Playing it where it lies

This means you can't move your ball to improve where it has come to rest.

Pro shop

The retail store for most courses, where the resident professional sells clubs, clothes, and balls and generally administers play and instruction.

Pull

A shot that goes left from the moment it is struck and remains left, not curving like a hook, but nonetheless still left.

Push

A shot that goes right from the moment it is struck and remains right, not curving like a slice, but nonetheless still right.

Relief
The rules allow you to move the ball in certain situations, thus getting relief from an unfair situation like having your ball sitting on a sprinkler head or a cart path.

Rough
The tall grass bordering the fairway.

Rule book
A list of the game's rules, compiled by the United States Golf Association here and by the Royal and Ancient Golf Club in Europe.

Sand wedge
A club designed specifically to get the ball out of a bunker or sand trap. A beefy flange on the club's bottom allows it to slide through sand.

Scramble
A game played by four people who continually use the best shot of the group. Also means to get out of trouble.

Shank
A shot that goes radically right, usually hit with a short iron. Normally the ball is struck by the area where the shaft joins the clubface.

Slice
The dread of most golfers, the slice goes right in the shape of a banana, costing accuracy and distance. Opposite of a hook.

Stance
The position of your body as you begin to strike the ball. It mostly has to do with the position of your feet and the alignment of your spine and shoulders.

Starter
The person who organizes play and gets golfers off in some kind of order, usually on a time table.

Starter set
An abbreviated set of clubs for the beginner, usually without as many irons and woods as are in a full 14-club set.

Stroke
The act of swinging the club with the intention of hitting the ball.

Tee
A three-inch wooden peg upon which your ball is placed in the hitting area at the start of each hole. Also called the tee box.

Tee box
Located at the start of each hole and defined by tee markers or blocks.

Unplayable
Sometimes a ball is so deep in the grass or bushes or trees that it cannot be hit and is thus declared unplayable and is allowed to be moved under the penalty of one stroke.

Up and down
The act of getting a chip or pitch shot up onto the green and close enough to the hole that the subsequent putt goes down, or into the hole.

Water hazard
An area defined by red or yellow stakes that is usually filled with water. The ball can be played from the area with no penalty, or removed at the cost of one penalty stroke.

Yips
A dastardly condition in putting in which a player is so fearful of the results that he or she makes a very jerky stroke.

index

A

accuracy, improving, 148

addressing the ball, 100

alignment

    defined, 192

    hook and, 156

    putting and, 141, 148, 163

amateurs, 8

approach shots, 11, 126–35

    defined, 192

Arizona, golf in, 185

Asia, golf in, 187

Augusta National Golf Course, 9

Australia, golf in, 187

B

back-nine contests, 70

backswing, 102–3, 105

    books about, 159

    for chip shot, 129

    improper, 158–59

    and slice, 155

bad shot, getting over, 167

bags, 91

    hard cases for traveling, 181

    pull carts, 66, 67

    Sunday bag, 66

    weight of, 66

balance, 100

ball, addressing the, 100

ball marker, 63, 139
    defined, 192
ball position, 101, 118, 119, 160
    for chip shot, 128, 129
    defined, 192
    for pitch shot, 130
balls, 86–87
    cost of, 86
    finding, 87
    having enough, 34, 52
    hitting too hard, 107
    identifying yours, 87
    lost, 59
    marking, 63, 139, 192
    not hitting squarely, 108
    out of bounds, 51, 59
    playing the wrong ball, 58
    provisional, 59
    used, 87
Bandon Dunes, Oregon, 190
barkie, 69
bee stings, 73
best-ball tournaments, 68
Bethpage State Park Golf Course, New York, 19,
        26
betting, 69, 174, 175
big dog. *See* drivers
birdie, 41
    defined, 192
blade putter, 84
bogey, 10, 40

    defined, 192
books
    backswing, 159
    chipping, 134
    course strategy and architecture, 53
    etiquette and rules, 35, 53, 75
    golf clubs, 93
    golf in general, 21, 93
    golf tips, 125
    guide to courses, 35
    history of golf, 111
    on majors, 21
    pitching, 134
    putting, 134, 151
    St. Andrews, 191
    swing, 111, 135
    tips from professionals, 177
    women golfers, 21, 35, 75, 93, 111
breaks, 140
British Open, 18
Brodie, John, 168
bunkers, 46, 50, 62
    defined, 192
    raking out sand, 58, 62
    sand shot, 132
business golf, 182

C

caddies, 19
carts, 64–65

at "public" private courses, 28, 29

required, 29

tournaments and, 67

using off the course, 65

cell phones, 61, 183

children

and driving ranges, 17

and golf, 8, 17

teaching golf to, 188–89

tournaments for junior golfers, 70

chili dip, 134

chippers, 135

chip shots, 128–29

books about, 134

defined, 192

on executive course, 27

mid-irons and, 131

versus pitch shots, 131

practicing, 170

closed clubface

defined, 192

and hook, 156

clothes, 52, 61, 90–91

club championship, 70

clubs, 12–13, 52. *See also* chippers; drivers; irons; putters; wedges; woods

books about, 93

buying new, 176

buying used, 92

buying your first set, 13, 92

loft of a club, 44, 78, 194

maximum allowed, 12, 183

perimeter-weighted, 80, 84, 194

"power fan," 135

regulation set, 12

rentals, 190

specialty clubs, 93

starter sets, 81, 92, 195

steel *versus* graphite shafts, 81

in titanium, 78, 92

travel bags for, 181

Web sites about, 92, 93

weight of, 66

Coeur d'Alene, Idaho, course, 32

community, golf and, 8

competitions. *See* tournaments

country clubs, 30–31

costs involved, 31

discriminating against women, 74

rule books, 57

couples tournaments, 70

course etiquette. *See* etiquette and rules

cup, 10

defined, 193

D

Decisions on the Rules of Golf (USGA), 56

difficult lies, 122

difficulty of courses

assessing, 29

at resorts, 33

Scottish and Irish courses, 187

divot, 52, 60, 120, 124
    defined, 193
    replacing, 62
dog-leg, 74, 169
    defined, 193
double bogey, 40
doublehanded grip, 98
downhill lie, 123
downswing, 102, 104–5
    increasing speed of, 105
draw, 156
    defined, 193
    versus hook, 157
dressing for the golf course, 52, 61, 90–91
drinking water, 72
drivers, 78, 79, 97
    defined, 193
    using, 96–97, 160
    woods used instead of, 96
driving ranges, 24–25
    and children, 17
    hi-tech ranges, 35
    indoor facilities, 24, 35
    practice at, 164
Dye, Pete, 39, 140

E

eagle, 41
equipment, 76–93
etiquette and rules, 34, 56–57
    beginners and, 52
    books on, 35, 53, 75
    justification, 57
    of putting, 138–39
    of the rough, 44
    unwritten, 60
Europe, golf in, 187
executive courses, 27

F

fade, defined, 193
fairways, 44–45, 112–25
    defined, 193
    driving on, 65
fairway woods, 79, 115
    defined, 193
fat
    defined, 193
    hitting, 160
feel
    defined, 193
    developing, 147, 149
first aid kit, 73
First Tee, The, organization, 189
flagstick, 63
    defined, 193
    tending, 139
flop shot, 133
Floyd, Raymond, 9
fluff, defined, 193

follow through, 102, 106–7

footwork, 107

"fore," 73

front-nine contests, 70

G

gambling, 69, 174, 175

game

  how it works, 10–11

  time spent on, 11

gap wedge, 82

gimme, 150

  defined, 193

gloves, 20, 61, 72, 89

  at driving range, 25

  for rain, 89, 124

golf anxiety, overcoming, 166–67

golf camps, 16, 189

golf courses, 36–53

  books, guides to, 35

  design, 39

  first American club, 9

  first time playing on, 20, 34

  hiring a pro to walk you around, 20

  length of, 38, 67

  maintenance of, 28

  number of holes, 38

  online guides to, 35, 75, 191

  par for the course, 40–41

  ratings, 29, 50–51

  repairing damage to, 62

  respecting the course, 62–63

  slope, 29, 50–51

Golf Digest, 33

Golf Magazine, 33

golf vacations, 16, 184–85

  Web sites on, 191

green. *See* putting greens

greens fee

  defined, 193

  at municipal courses, 26, 34

  at "public" private courses, 28

grip, 98–99, 109

  for fairway woods, 119

  hook and, 156

  interlocking, 98

  for irons, 119

  putting and, 142

  weakness in, 154

H

half short, 165

half swing, 130

handicap, 14–15, 173

  handicap certificate, 14, 15

  scratch, 15

hats, 72

Hawaii, golf in, 185

hazards, 46–47. *See also* sand traps;
    water hazards

height of player, 111

history of golf, 9

Hogan, Ben, 124
hole, 10
hook, 108
    defined, 193
    fixing, 156–57

I

improving your game, 152–77
interlocking grip, 98
Ireland, golf in, 186–87
irons, 80–81, 114–15
    defined, 193
    3-iron, 125
    5-iron, 124
    8-iron, 116, 124, 128
    9-iron, 116
    long irons, 114, 115
    mid-irons, 114, 131
    short irons, 114, 116–17, 128, 131

J

James II of Scotland, 9
Jones, Bobby, 9
Jones, Robert Trent, Sr., 39
Jones, Robert Trent, Trail, Alabama, 185

K

Kraft Nabisco Championship, 19

L

Ladies Professional Golf Association, 9
Las Vegas, courses in, 33
left-handed players, 93
left-hand low grip, 142
Leonard, Justin, 124
lessons, 16–17, 96, 176. *See also* teaching pros
    to fix a slice, 154
    group lessons, 17
    importance of, 20
    before playing on a course, 34
    where to take, 34
lies
    difficult, 122
    downhill, 123
    side-hill, 123
    tight, 122
    unplayable, 134
    uphill, 123
line, defined, 194
lining up your shot, 100
links golf, 186
lob wedge, 82, 83, 131
    defined, 194
loft, 44, 78
    defined, 194
long irons, 114
    fairway woods compared to, 115
long putter, 85
    awkwardness of, 150
long putts, 146

developing feel on, 149

practicing, 170

LPGA Championship, 19

M

Mackenzie, Alister, 39

magazines

golf for women, 19

resort golf courses, 33

Mangum, Geoff, 151

Masters Championship, 9, 18

matchplay, 56

defined, 194

measuring distance to the green, 121

medal play, defined, 194

Member-Guest tournament, 70

Member-Member tournament, 70

mental tips, 168–69

metal woods, defined, 194

mid-irons, 114

for chipping, 131

miniature golf, 17

Morris, Old Tom, 39

mulligans, 177

municipal courses, 26–27

greens fees at, 26, 34

proving residency, 27

walking, 67

munis. *See* municipal courses

muscle memory, 164

Myrtle Beach, South Carolina, courses in, 33, 185

N

Nassau, 68, 172, 174

defined, 194

$2 Nassau, 68

Nelson, Byron, 124

New Zealand, courses in, 187

Nicklaus, Jack, 9

My Golden Lessons, 177

19th hole, 30

Norman, Greg, 9

O

Okanagan, British Columbia, courses in, 33, 185

Old Course (St. Andrews, Scotland), 186

one-piece takeaway, 102, 158

open, defined, 194

out-of-bounds ball, 51, 59

P

pacing yourself, 53, 61, 150

Palmer, Arnold, 9

par

for the course, 40–41

defined, 10, 194

determining, 41

making par on a hole, 11

personal par, 40

par-3 holes, 40

number on a course, 52

pro's tips for, 37, 154

par-4 holes, 40
    number on a course, 52
    pro's tips for, 23, 55, 77, 95, 113, 137, 179
par-5 holes, 41
    difficulty of, 40
    number on a course, 52
    pro's tips for, 7
paralysis by analysis, 176
Pebble Beach, California, courses in, 26, 185
penalty strokes, 58
    for ball out of bounds, 51, 59
    defined, 194
    for hitting another ball on the green, 139
    unplayable lies and, 134
    water hazards and, 46, 50
perimeter-weighted clubs
    defined, 194
    irons, 80
    putters, 84
personal par, 40
PGA Championship, 18
Phoenix, Arizona, courses in, 33
pin. *See* flagstick
Pinehurst, North Carolina, courses in, 185
pitching wedge, 82, 131
    and chip shot, 128
    defined, 194
pitch shots, 27, 130–31
    books about, 134
    versus chip shots, 131
    clubs for, 131
    defined, 194

playing against yourself, 8
playing it where it lies, 58
    defined, 194
positioning the ball. *See* ball position
power fan, 135
practice
    how to, 164–65
    and lowering your score, 170
    practice swings, 110
    practicing the way you play, 165
    putting, 149, 162
    at a range, 25
    and sand traps, 133
    short game, 165, 170
    and slice, 155
Price, Nick, 9
Professional Golfers Association, 16
professional golf tournaments, 18–19
    going to a, 187
pros. *See* teaching pros
pro shop, defined, 194
pro's tips
    par 3, difficult, 37
    par 3, easy, 154
    par 4, difficult, 55, 113
    par 4, easy, 23, 77
    par 4, moderate, 95, 137, 179
    par 4, very difficult, 127
    par 5, difficult, 7
public courses. *See* municipal courses
"public" private courses, 28–29
pull, 109, 155

defined, 194

pull carts, 66, 67
   battery-powered, 67

push, 109, 157
   defined, 194

putters, 84–85, 93
   long putter, 85, 150
   using putter to read the green, 48

putting, 136–51
   anxiety and, 49, 145
   books about, 134, 151
   controlling direction, 151
   controlling distance, 146
   etiquette and rules, 60, 138–39
   lining up, 140
   long putts, 146, 149, 170
   poor putting, 162
   practice, 149
   short putts, 163, 170

putting greens, 10, 48–49
   breaks in, 140
   defined, 193
   marking ball on, 63
   measuring distance to, 121
   slope, 48
   water hazards around, 47

R

rain, playing in the, 117, 124
   gloves for, 89, 124

"read the green," 48

red stakes, 47

relief, 58
   defined, 195

rescue clubs, 93

reserving tee time
   at municipal courses, 26, 27
   at "public" private courses, 29

resort golf courses, 32–33
   difficulty of, 33

respect
   for the course, 62–63
   while playing golf, 21

reverse pivot, 160

Robert Trent Jones Trail, Alabama, 185

romance of golf, 8–9

rough, 44
   defined, 195

Royal and Ancient Golf Club (St. Andrews, Scotland), 9

rule book, defined, 195

rules. *See* etiquette and rules

Rules of Golf, The (USGA), 56

S

safety, 72–73

St. Andrews, Scotland, 9, 186, 191

St. George, Utah, 33

sandbaggers, 15

sandie, 69

sand traps, 46, 50, 62
   raking out, 58, 62

sand shot, 132

sand wedge, 82, 83, 131, 132–33

   and chip shot, 128

   defined, 195

score, lowering your, 170–71

scorekeeping, 11, 15

   in best-ball tournaments, 68

   good score, 74

Scotch Ball, 71

Scotland, courses in, 9, 186–87, 191

scrambles, 68, 172

   defined, 195

scratch, 15

setup, slice and, 155

shank, defined, 195

shoes, 20, 52, 88

   at driving range, 25

   replacing spikes on, 88

short game practice, 165, 170

short irons, 114, 116–17

   and chip shot, 128, 131

short putts, 163

   practicing, 170

shot, visualizing the, 168–69

side-hill lie, 123

Singh, Vijay, 125

single player, 180

sky ball, 161

slice, 108

   defined, 195

   fixing, 154–55, 176

slope of course, 29, 50–51

slope of putting green, 48

Snead, Sam, 99

socializing, 21

Sorenstam, Annika, 9

specials, 175

speed, putting and, 141

stance, 100–101

   closed, 101

   defined, 195

   putting and, 142

   when using irons, 118–19

starter, defined, 195

storms, 73

stroke play, 56

strokes, 10. *See also* penalty strokes

   counting, 51

   defined, 195

"sudden death," 74–75

sunscreen, 72

swing, 120–21

   books about, 111, 135

   difficulty in mastering, 110

   fit of clubs and, 13

   improving, 135

   inside out or outside in, 108

T

takeaway, one-piece, 102, 158

tall grass, 122

target golf, 39

target line, 101

teaching pros. *See also* lessons
  at country clubs, 30
  finding, 16
  for help with slicing and hooking, 109
  walking you around the course, 20
tee, 10, 42–43, 52
  defined, 195
  height at which to tee ball, 97
tee box
  choosing the right one, 42
  defined, 195
teeing off, 94–112
  first player, 60, 61
  tee-off error, 108–9
tee markers, 97
  color coding, 42, 43
tee time, 26
  reserving, 26, 27, 29
television and golf, 9
three-jack, 163
tight lie, 122
topping the ball, 161
tournaments
  best-ball, 68
  country clubs, 70–71
  couples, 70
  dos and don'ts, 172–73
  golf carts at, 67
  local matches, 68–69
  types of, 56
  for women, 74
traveling

  with clubs, 181
  golf and, 180, 190
trees, purpose of, 45
Trevino, Lee, 9, 156

U

United States Golf Association (USGA), 9
  and handicap, 14
  and ratings of golf courses, 51
unplayable lies, 134
  defined, 195
up and down, defined, 195
uphill lies, 123
USGA. *See* United States Golf Association
U.S. Open, 9, 18
  2002, 19, 26
U.S. Women's Open, 19

V

Vardon grip, 98, 99
video recorder and teaching golf, 16
visualizing the shot, 168–69

W

walking the course, 26, 66–67
  versus riding in a cart, 34
warming up, 72
water hazards, 46, 50
  defined, 195

hitting, 167

Watson, Tom, 9

Webb, Karrie, 9

Web sites
  buying and selling club memberships, 35, 75
  buying used clubs, 92
  on clubs, 93
  general, 21, 111
  golf mall, 93
  golf resorts, 33
  golf tips, 125
  golf vacations, 191
  guide to courses, 35, 75, 191
  putting, 151
  rules and etiquette, 35, 53, 75
  St. Andrews golf, 191
  tips from professionals, 177
  women golfers, 35, 75

wedges, 82–83, 93
  lob, 82, 83, 131, 194
  pitching, 82, 128, 131, 194
  sand, 82, 83, 128, 131, 132–33, 195

weight transfer, 119

where to play, 22–35

wind, playing in the, 117, 124

winter rules, 59, 75

women
  American players, 9
  books for, 21, 35, 75, 93, 111
  country clubs and, 74
  magazines for, 19
  professional tournaments, 19
  tournaments for, 74
  using woods, 92
  Web sites for, 35, 75

Women's British Open, 19

woods, 78–79
  lofted metal woods, 93
  used instead of driver, 96
    3-wood, 92, 96
    5-wood, 96

Woods, Tiger, 9, 17, 53, 80
  How I Play Golf, 111, 159

Y

yardage book, 29

yearly fee
  at country clubs, 31
  at municipal courses, 27

yellow stakes, 47

yips, defined, 195

Z

Zagat Golf Guides, 33

Zaharias, Babe, 9

ABOUT THE AUTHOR

Blaine Newnham is a sports columnist and associate editor for *The Seattle Times*. While he writes about a number of major sports, golf remains his favorite. He has covered all the top players from Ben Hogan at the 1966 U.S. Open to Tiger Woods at all four of his consecutive major championship wins in 2000 and 2001. He has been playing golf for nearly 50 years and currently has a handicap index of 13.9 (you can look it up). He lives in Indianola, Washington, with his wife, Joanna.

Silver Lining Books would also like to thank the following consultants for their help in preparing this book: **Carl Alexander,** Director of Golf at GlenArbor Golf Club in Bedford, New York; **Steve Archer,** Head Golf Professional at Quail Valley Golf Club in Vero Beach, Florida; **Ted Eletheriou,** Eastern Regional Director of Nike Golf Learning Centers; **David Tunkkari,** the Head Golf Professional at Wing Point Golf and Country Club, Bainbridge Island, Washington; **Sean Parees,** Head Golf Professional at Quicksilver Golf Club, Midway, Pennsylvania. Silver Lining Books would also like to thank **Dave Morgan** and **Peter Livingston** for their guidance in the development of this book.

Barbara J. Morgan Publisher, Silver Lining Books

Barnes & Noble Basics
Barb Chintz Editorial Director
Leonard Vigliarolo Design Director

Barnes & Noble Basics *Golf*™
Lorraine Iannello Managing Editor
Barbara Rietschel Art Director
Elizabeth McNulty Editorial Production Coordinator
Leslie Stem Design Assistant
Monique Boniol Picture Researcher
Emily Seese Editorial Assistant
Della R. Mancuso Production Manager

Photo Credits: Adams Golf: 12, 80; Artville: 31, 39, 69, 145; Bettmann Archive/Corbis: 9; Colonial Country Club: 7, 23, 37, 55, 77, 95, 113, 127, 137, 153, 169, 179; Columbia ParCar Corp.: 65 Dart Drake; Comstock: 70, 81, 98, 185; Corbis: cover Chuck Savage, 1, 8, 10 Michael Brennan, 14, 28, 32, 40, 42, 44, 45, 46, 48, 49, 56, 58, 59, 60, 63, 68, 71, 88, 89, 91, 96, 97, 116, 117, 120, 122, 138, 141, 142, 144, 147, 148, 162, 164, 189 ©Royalty Free, 166, 168, 170, 172 Rolf Bruderer, 174, 180, 182 R. W. Jones, 184 Kit Kittle, 188; Fair & Green Apparel: 90 Peter Baker Studio; Getty Images: 26 Photodisc, 62 Paul Severn; Golf Academy at The Golf Club at Chelsea Pier: 24; *Golf Magazine*: 18, 30, and 39 Fred Vuich, 100, 102, 103, 104, and 106 Cheryl Anderson, 107 Keiichi Sato, 119 Sam Greenwood; Hill Billy USA: 66; Kiawah Island Golf Resort: 47, 50; Robert Malazzo:16, 128, 129, 130, 131; Matzie Golf Company: 98; Never Compromise: 85; Ogio International, Inc.: 181; Ping: 83, 84 right, 91; Sally Mara Sturman: 13, 43, 72, 78, 82, 99, 108, 114, 115, 118, 132, 134, 140, 154, 156, 160; Sun Mountain Sports, Inc.: 67; Titleist: 79, 84 left; www.golfvacations.com: 191; www.standrews.org.uk: 186 Chris Hughes